Praise for *Mindful Eating 101*

"*Mindful Eating 101* is the perfect resource for the incredibly difficult obstacle of learning to trust ourselves when it comes to a relationship with our bodies and food. I hope that this book becomes MANDATORY reading for anyone entering into that phase of their life."

— **Jamie-Lynn Sigler,** star of *The Sopranos*, author of *Wise Girl: What I've Learned About Life, Love, and Loss*

"Let *Mindful Eating 101* allow you the freedom to enjoy one of the most incredible times of your life without the confusion and frustration that mind*less* eating can bring!"

— **Emme,** supermodel, television personality, and best-selling author

"An insightful guide to a very sensitive issue. Dr. Albers does a wonderful job of guiding college students to a healthier lifestyle and positive self-esteem. I wish this book had been available when I was a college student."

— **Beth Shaw**, founder and president of YogaFit Inc.

What the professionals are saying

"Dr. Albers has done a brilliant job targeting both obvious and subtle issues specific to college life and outlining ways to recognize, prepare for, and overcome mindless overeating pitfalls. This vitally important work should be required reading for every student stepping onto a college campus!"

— **Denise Lamothe, Psy.D., HHD**, author of *The Taming of the Chew: A Holistic Guide to Stopping Compulsive Eating*

"Written in an accessible and practical manner, readers learn life lessons about their relationship with food, their bodies, and their spirit that will last long after their final semester ends. *Mindful Eating 101* should be required reading for students of all ages!"

— **Kathleen Burns Kingsbury, LMHC**, co-author, *Weight Wisdom: Affirmations to Free You from Food and Body Concerns*

"Susan Albers's incredibly thoughtful book reminds us that self-care and self-love are necessary tools in our everyday lives. She guides us gently to a place of greater understanding and ignites in readers a sense of true empowerment."

— **Jessica Weiner**, author of *Do I Look Fat in This?* and *A Very Hungry Girl*

What the students are saying

"*Mindful Eating 101* is an accessible guide to lifetime eating that speaks to our generation as it approaches eating holistically—through the mind and soul. This is not just another self-help book; it's a work that truly wants to better women's approaches to eating in college and forevermore."

— **Meg Lyons,** Colgate University senior

"Dr. Albers captures the everyday life of the average student in a funny and insightful way. The book is sort of self-help-meets-the-diet-world; it forces us to look at food and 'mindful eating' as part of the overall college experience, not merely as an accessory to it."

— **Katie Goldstein,** University of Vermont sophomore

Mindful Eating 101

A GUIDE

TO

HEALTHY EATING

IN

COLLEGE

AND

BEYOND

Susan Albers, Psy.D.

Routledge
Taylor & Francis Group
NEW YORK AND LONDON

Published in 2006 by
Routledge
Taylor & Francis Group
711 Third Avenue,
New York, NY 10017, USA

Published in Great Britain by
Routledge
2 Park Square
Milton Park, Abingdon
Oxfordshire OX14 4RN

First issued in hardback 2016

Routledge is an imprint of the Taylor & Francis Group, an informa business

International Standard Book Number-13: 978-1-138-17231-9 (hbk)
International Standard Book Number-13: 978-0-415-95093-0 (Softcover)
Library of Congress Card Number 2005020805

Library of Congress Cataloging-in-Publication Data

Albers, Susan, Psy.D.
Mindful eating 101 : a guide to healthy eating in college and beyond / Susan Albers.
p. cm.
Includes bibliographical references.
ISBN 0-415-95093-7 (pbk.)
1. College students-Nutrition. 2. College students-Health and hygiene. 3. Nutrition.
I. Title: Mindful eating one hundred one. II. Title.

RA777.3.A43 2006
613--dc22 2005020805

I dedicate this book to all institutions of higher learning:
May you teach your students to nurture
their *bodies* every bit as well as their *minds*

—Susan Albers Psy.D.

"The mind is like an umbrella—it only works when it is open."

Sir James Jeans, Scientist (1877–1946)

Contents

Preface
The Mindful Eating Syllabus

Imagine for a moment that you are sitting on the set of a popular daytime talk show. The show's theme today is "The Dining Hall Romance: Surviving Your Love–Hate Relationship with Food." If you are a college student, it is a pretty safe bet that you love to eat, but detest the dorm food. Although the cafeteria and unlimited buffets leave much to be desired, you find yourself mindlessly eating. In other words, you order pizza late at night even when you aren't hungry, stress eat before big exams, and have resorted to dieting. You wish someone would just tell you what to eat so you wouldn't have to worry about it. But you do worry about it. You earnestly wonder why some days you eat healthy foods and other days you eat junk. Then, you begin a cycle of dieting and punishing your body with grueling workouts. If this sounds familiar, you have experienced the challenges of mindless eating first hand. Unfortunately, you are a self-taught expert on rocky romances with food and mindless eating.

Today, you have been invited to be a special guest on the show to share your mindless eating expertise. As the program returns from a commercial break and the music dies down, the host leans toward you. She asks compassionately: "I wonder why mindless eating has become such an issue for you in college. A great deal of your time is invested in thinking about food, studying calories, stressing out about your weight, and checking for hints of cellulite in mirrors."

It's true. You've tried to get out of the mindless eating cycle. Your bookshelf is full of the latest diet craze books. But after a few days of dieting, you fell right back into your mindless eating habits. Did you feel thinner or happier? No. Why do dieting books make managing your weight look so easy?

Everyone in the audience can identify with your mindless eating struggle. It really doesn't matter who you are, one thing we all know is that there is a fine line between eating too much and too little. There is an even finer line between loving and hating your body. It's likely that you will cross that line many, many times in your life. A significant number of people take their first step toward mindless eating during college. Unfortunately, these first steps toward mindless eating can damage healthy eating patterns for many years to come or for a lifetime.

Consider right now what you would tell the TV host. Would you confess that you are a mindless eater who worries about gaining the "freshman fifteen?" Perhaps you are still searching for a miracle diet, one that will magically melt off the pounds and make you look like a model. Do you feel guilty because you are "cheating" on your diet with your favorite foods—corned beef on warm rye bread with thick, creamy Russian dressing, and a piece of freshly baked blueberry pie? Perhaps you have even wondered whether you have an eating problem. If you can relate to these sentiments, this book is for you.

Are You a Mindless Eater?

Examine the following list. You might be a mindless eater if you:

- Worry about gaining the "freshman fifteen" or gaining weight
- Overeat to the point of feeling too full
- Find yourself saying that you are too busy to eat or not making meals a priority (skipping or eating on the run)
- Eat because you are under pressure (i.e., eating a bag of chips while writing a term paper that is due in four hours)
- Notice that you think a lot about food
- Wonder if you have a truly "healthy" relationship with food
- Diet unsuccessfully
- Experience ups and downs in your weight
- Want to learn how to improve your self-esteem
- Say "I feel fat!"
- Think you are overweight

- Know someone who has eating and body image issues and want to learn more
- Want to help yourself or someone else develop a more mindful relationship to food
- Obsess about your image in the mirror

If you answered "yes" to one or more of these, keep reading.

Welcome

Welcome to *Mindful Eating 101*. If you are a soon-to-be college student, currently enrolled in school or are a graduate student, it is truly worth your time to read through this book and study up on healthy ways to navigate college cafeterias, avoid mindless late night snacking, and cope with troubling eating habits. Believe me, there is no better investment in your future than a stellar education in mindful eating, the art of eating in an aware, nourishing, and satisfying manner. Granted, you didn't come to college to learn how to eat, a skill you believed you'd mastered before the first day of kindergarten. But, perhaps you hit a few roadblocks in your healthy eating habits. Self-doubt, low self-esteem, unrealistic expectations, perfectionism, body dissatisfaction, and eating issues are just a few barriers to healthy, mindful eating.

These roadblocks are part of the "too plus too" dilemma. Too fat, too skinny, too tall, too whatever. "Too plus too" basically equals "four-get" feeling good about yourself. Our brains seem programmed to judge our bodies on the ideals of society. We aren't taught that beauty comes in many shapes and sizes and that the uniqueness of each individual should be celebrated. No one ever models how to feel good enough exactly as you are. Everyone wants to be smarter, richer, happier, more attractive and most of all thinner. Maybe you have said to yourself, "If only I could lose that last five pounds, then I would feel more confident in this dress and happier about myself." It's not healthy to tie happiness to thinness, but most of us do. That is why it is so easy to be sucked into trying fad diets. We all know it is important to be healthy, happy, and comfortable with yourself—whether you are a size two or a size eighteen. How to get there is another matter.

Mindful eating helps you overcome these "too plus too" problems. It teaches you how to be introspective, nonjudgmental, aware, and accepting of yourself. You use these skills to make wise, healthy decisions to nourish and feed your body. You'd think that eating mindfully should be a snap, but it is a very challenging task to master. You must embrace the inner struggles of eating mindfully. Be patient while you learn how to restructure your eating patterns.

Instructions for Reading This Book

For a short time, put aside everything that you've learned in fashion magazines and dieting books. Get rid of the articles that start out "lose five pounds in ten days." Keep an open mind. To eat mindfully, there is no menu or particular foods to avoid, such as carbohydrates or fats. In fact, it isn't even about what to eat or not to eat. Instead, it is a crash course on training your mind how to think about the "where," "what," and "why" you eat. For this reason, the techniques will seem curious and foreign to you. The goal is to understand *why* you eat. It's as simple as that. Once you know what factors prompt you to stop or start eating, you will know what makes you more vulnerable to mindless eating patterns. Mindful eating aims to give you a greater sense of control and tranquility at meals.

So many diet plans fail because they are not realistically tailored to one's lifestyle. If you've ever tried to cut out carbohydrates when pasta and bagels were a staple of your diet, you know what I mean. When people blindly adhere to a diet plan without adapting it to their lifestyle, culture, or favorite foods, it simply doesn't work. It is impossible for many busy medical, law, or dental students to spend hours in the kitchen preparing special diet meals. Some diets rely on expensive foods like salmon and steak that students on a budget cannot afford. You have heard of the diets that demand bacon and eggs for breakfast everyday. What if you don't like bacon and eggs—or the thought of such a repetitive dining choice is not attractive to you? The college diner will fail because the expectations set by many diet plans are unhealthy, unrealistic, time consuming, or financially burdensome.

You might think that healthy eating takes away the college perks, but it doesn't. You can still enjoy popcorn and nachos at sorority meetings, pizza and a movie on Saturday night in the dorm lounge, and tea and cookies at the library hosted by the senior faculty. Diets tell you to avoid; mindful eating teaches you how to moderate.

Sadly, some diets are the beginning of dangerous and disorderly habits. Most people eventually drop restrictive meal plans. But, some people get really good at jumping through the unrealistic hoops set up by the diet. This can lead to long-term problematic eating.

I recommend that you read the entire book before you begin your journey into mindful eating. Mindfulness is a serious endeavor that can lead you to change your eating patterns for the rest of your life. Take some time to reflect, reread the chapters, and do the homework assignments relevant to you.

The benefit of a book like this is that it is flexible and easily adapted to the busy lifestyle of a college student. The downside is that it is inevitably a general treatment of the subject. A book that considered every nuance of mindless eating couldn't possibly fit between two covers. I do not prescribe foods or tell you what to have for breakfast. I am telling you a better way to *think* about eating.

I've Already Tried to Eat More Mindfully

What stands in the way of mindful eating? People give many reasons and excuses for their mindless eating habits. One of the most common rationales given for paying little attention to one's eating habits is lack of time. College students are swamped with club meetings, research papers, work-study obligations, and relationships. The good news is that mindful eating does not take time away from classes, parties, or homework. So, if busyness was your excuse, this is a good book for you because it doesn't require two hours sweating in the gym.

Share Your Mindful Eating Habits

Perhaps the most valuable thing you can do is to share the book, examples, and tips with your friends, roommates, classmates, professors, therapist, and college counseling center. When you start talking about it, you will be surprised how many people will admit, "Oh yes, I struggle with mindless eating too." If you are in a social club where you notice an undercurrent of self-esteem problems, food anxiety and weight issues, consider bringing this book to the attention of the club members.

Mindful Eating Is for Everyone

For many years, society has wrongly believed that only women worry about their weight and mindless eating habits. This stereotype is long gone and is practically ancient history. It's true that women out number men with eating issues by a ratio of ten to one. However, the prevalence of men with eating concerns is growing (O'Dea and Abraham 2002; Jacobi 2005). Or, men have had eating issues in the past that were hidden and not discussed in public. Today, men's eating concerns are gaining more attention in the public, clinical research, and coverage by the media.

So, this book is for *anyone* with an eating issue. It doesn't matter if you are male or female, and neither ethnicity nor race are a factor. Everyone can learn to eat a little more mindfully. In fact, since there are no menus, you can tailor these ideas to the foods you traditionally eat in your culture. Whether it's shepherd's pie, Pad Thai, a cheeseburger, a knish, tofu, or paella, you can learn how to mindfully eat it.

The Mindful Eating Warning Label

It is imperative that you closely read appendix A, which focuses on finding additional help and counseling, if you've had a history of eating disorder or are currently experiencing one or more of the following symptoms:

- purging
- severe binge eating
- depression
- very low calorie intake
- harming yourself in any way
- suicidal thoughts
- abusing any substances
- feeling fat when others tell you that you are too thin
- physical symptoms such as feeling faint, underweight, stomach pain, irregular or no menstrual period, sore throat, etc.
- eating concerns or body image interfering with relationships and/or academic/work performance

You may or may not have an eating problem that needs attention. Only a mental health clinician or physician can do an assessment and determine what kind of assistance you may need. This book is not a substitute for treatment.

> ***Welcome, Mindful Eating 101:*** According to the old proverb, give a man a fish and he eats for a day; teach a man to fish and he eats for a lifetime. My contemporary version goes something like this: Give students a diet book and they eat low carb or fat free in the cafeteria for a week. Educate students on the ancient art of mindfulness and they will learn a lifetime of mindful eating.

So, please join this class on mindful eating. Again, welcome and enjoy!

Acknowledgments

I am deeply indebted to my clients and the college students who graciously contributed their thoughts, stories, and quotes to this book. Thank you for candidly sharing your mindful eating journey. The students who read this book will greatly benefit from your insights and examples.

While working on this book, I couldn't help but call to mind my own college memories. A heartfelt thanks to all my College of Wooster friends who reminisced with me as I wrote this book: Jane Lindquist, Eric Lingenfelter, John Bowling, Brian Kayla, Betsy Beyer, Amy Clatworthy, and J.T. Krohe, as well as a variety of "Betas" and the "Shearer House women." I'd like to express my appreciation of Dr. Jason Greif, who was my classmate at the University of Denver, and Giti Pieper for her friendship during my postdoctoral fellowship at Stanford University.

Thanks to the dedicated prodding of Mrs. Baird, my teacher and first writing coach, and the Wertz family for their college advice. I am forever grateful for the connections I made in Denver, which taught me how to truly enjoy life and be in the moment. Lynne Knobloch-Fedders and Carl Fedders, I am appreciative of your friendship and invaluable assistance setting up my Web site.

Thank you to Dr. Luis G. Manzo for reviewing my manuscripts. Dr. Manzo's professional feedback, suggestions, and cheerleading were always amazingly helpful. I'd also like to acknowledge my editors and reviewers at Routledge and New Harbinger Publications for publishing my first book, *Eating Mindfully: How to End Mindless Eating and Develop a Balanced Relationship with Food.* Also, a special thank you to the staff at the Women's Health Center, a branch of the Cleveland Clinic Foundation, the University of Notre Dame Counseling Center, The Stanford University Counseling and Psychological Services, and Ohio Wesleyan University Counseling Center.

I am forever mindful of the support and encouragement of my family. Carmela Albers always has her suitcase packed at a moment's notice to attend my Mindful Eating Workshops. Thank you to Dr. Thomas Albers for his adventurous attitude of "try it, you might like it," and to Rhonda, John, and Jimmer Bowling for their encouragement. I am particularly grateful to J.R., for his support and for sharing many mindful meals with me at Beuhlers, our favorite place. Thanks to Linda Serotta for exploring Japan with me twice and for diligently reviewing my manuscript. I am also thankful to have Jenna, Paul, and Judd Serotta as part of the family. To the newest Dr. Albers—Dr. Angie Albers—thanks for the late night consultations and humorous insights. I am so grateful to Dr. Victoria Gould for our frequent personal and professional chats and her unique talent of "getting me" with having to say almost no words at all.

Introduction
The Food Fight

"Fooood fight!" These two words launched one of the best known cafeteria food fights ever filmed—in a scene from *Animal House,* a 1978 campus comedy. The food fight scene has become a classic, setting the tone for many other college movies that parody student life. Today, the food fight scene still makes many people laugh. However, this film footage unfortunately embodies many of the negative stereotypes about college food and students' unhealthy eating habits that we still hold today. Students are labeled as mindless overeaters who overload on junk food and unhealthy snacks, clueless when it comes to healthy eating. Granted, student's eating habits already had this reputation long before Animal House was ever shown, but over the intervening decades this image still remains.

"Guess What I Am?"

Let's take a closer look at what actually sparked the infamous food fight in *Animal House.* Bluto, the main character, played by John Belushi, enters the college dining hall. The camera shadows Bluto as he begins mindlessly eating as he walks down the cafeteria line. He starts by stuffing a pastry into his mouth all the while shoving sandwiches and a variety of other foods into his pockets. Then, he gobbles up a portion of a hamburger and inhales some Jell-O. He keeps eating, even as he piles food on his tray. With a heaping tray, he plops down at a table next to his fraternity brother, Otter. He never takes a break to even chew or taste the food. It's the epitome of mindless eating.

Bluto would raise a few eyebrows if he was spotted in a cafeteria line today. The food he rapidly inhales during this episode would spark a variety of questions and concerns. Was Bluto just mindlessly eating or does he have a serious food issue? Other students might recall seeing him in the dining hall on previous occasions to determine if this is typical behavior or not. Is his behavior a matter of concern? Is this a sign that he needs help? It is impossible to tell just by looking, whether or not a person has a mindful relationship with food or if a mindless eating episode signals a significant problem.

Movie viewers are perfectly aware that Bluto's mindless eating is simply used in the movie to exaggerate and poke fun at the freedom students experience in college. They can eat what they please, healthy or not. There is no parent standing over them saying, "You'll spoil your dinner" or "Eat your peas!" But, the other characters in the movie aren't privy to this joke and don't really know why he is eating so strangely and mindlessly.

Rather than voicing a concern or curiosity about Bluto, a woman watching him does what many of us do when we are uncomfortable or confused by someone else's behavior, we judge. As Bluto mindlessly sucks up the food, she sneers "P.I.G." down her nose. Bluto ignores her and replies, "See if you can guess what I am now." He stuffs mashed potatoes and gravy into his mouth until his cheeks are full. He hits both his cheeks and sprays potatoes all over the disgusted, horrified onlookers. "I'm a zit," he announces happily. "Get it?" It is as a result of this gross, immature joke that a massive food fight erupts.

Since Animal House, we have continued to be bombarded with images and messages that students are mindless eaters. The term freshman fifteen has single handedly convinced many students that healthy eating is not the norm. Newspaper and magazine articles point to the social and health consequences of mindless eating. Students are adamantly warned to be wary of mindless eating in college. However, simply pointing out that freshmen tend to gain weight doesn't prevent it from happening.

Why Are Students Labeled as Mindless Eaters?

Unlimited buffet lines, greasy junk food, and mindless eating are most often the reasons used to explain the majority of students' unhealthy eating habits and the curiously high prevalence of eating issues among students. If dining halls were to blame for students' eating problems, the issue would be easy to fix—dining hall cuisine would be made healthier and the problem would be eliminated. But mindless eating and disordered eating habits are highly complex health and psychological issues that affect many students throughout the nation, not to mention the majority of the population at large (Cooley and Toray 1996; Hoerr, Bokram, Lugo, Bivins, and Keast 2002).

Clearly this epidemic of eating problems is about much more than greasy fries, unlimited buffets, and grilled cheese sandwiches. How can colleges tackle an entire culture that continually presents unhealthy body images in the media? How can colleges help students to reduce stress to manageable levels so that the traditional developmental hurdles of college life are easier to negotiate? Undoubtedly, the psychological and social pressures of college life, combined with unhealthy dining options are both key factors. Even the most mindful of eaters can have a difficult time eating in a healthy manner whilst they are in college.

Improvements in Campus Dining

In the early twenty-first century, there is a refreshing new attitude about the importance of healthy food in college. Sure, there are still cafeterias with unlimited buffets and fattening, unhealthy food options. However, there are also food courts, organic food, vegetarian and vegan options, healthy fast food, and structured food point plans tailored to individual needs.

Quality food and healthy eating habits are finally being granted the attention they deserve. Academic institutions know that the fuel students put in their bodies affects academic output and quality of life.

Institutions of higher learning are recognizing that they have a prime responsibility to create a mindful and healthy environment. While many dining halls and catering services are making a concerted effort, there is still an important piece missing. It's not only a question of getting rid of the wilted lettuce and overcooked burgers: Students have to be taught how to moderate their eating, no matter what they eat. Serving top of the line gourmet meals doesn't assist students in overcoming stress eating, neither does it help them to ignore social pressure to be thin, to manage portion sizes, or alleviate their guilt when they mindlessly eat off the gourmet dessert bar.

Today, many institutions of higher learning across the country are incorporating healthy eating into their cafeterias. For example, Dartmouth College in New Hampshire, has an innovative dining option called Home Plate, which offers a wide range of healthy foods, such as salad, a potato bar, low cholesterol stir fry, grilled salmon, and gardenburgers. The College of Wooster, a liberal arts college in Ohio, has a cafeteria with a "no fry zone" that avoids serving the typical college fare of french fries and deep fried onion rings. Stanford University Law School's café has such healthy snacks as organic cookies, curried tofu, and sushi on its menu. Many colleges are following suit.

The Current Food Fight

For today's men and women the battleground is entirely within the confines of their own heads. Students quarrel fiercely with themselves about their eating habits. They are constantly wondering whether they're eating too much, whether they are getting fat, or whether their bodies are okay. Like the majority of the population, students also buy the idea that one must have a flawless, perfect body to be really successful, to feel good, and be happy. The pressure and expectations don't help anyone to eat more mindfully.

Mindless Eating Doesn't Get Enough Attention

Eating disorders on college campuses get a lot of press. For this reason, few people realize that mindless eating problems are far more prevalent than medically defined eating disorders, which occur in a small group as compared to the entire student population (Heatherton, Nichols, Mahamedi, and Keel 1995; Hoerr, Bokram, Lugo, Bivins, and Keast 2002; Parham, Lennon, and Kolosi 2001). The majority of college students struggle with mindless overeating, dieting, skimping on meals, body image worries, have strict food rules, or do not eat enough to get adequate nutrition. Studies indicate that between 45 and 73 percent of college students have tried dieting with an even larger number, 30 to 70 percent, are thought to have significantly disordered eating (Hendricks et al. 2004; Hoyt and Ross 2003; Mintz and Betz 1988; Clayton et al. 1997; Snelling, Schaeffer, and Lehrhoff 2002). "Disordered eating," doesn't meet the full diagnostic criteria specified by the American Psychological association to be considered a psychological and medical "disorder." However, disordered eating involves habits that are distressing enough to significantly interfere with academic work, health, relationships, and social life (Cooley and Toray 1996).

What's the Harm in Dieting?

Many mindless eaters try dieting for the first time in college. Some dieters lose weight in the short term, others gain weight, and some find their weight remains unchanged. So, what's the problem with dieting? For most people, a diet is quickly dropped, and in most cases it doesn't enable them to develop long lasting, mindful eating skills.

For others, fad diets chart a course toward very problematic eating. For these individuals, dieting teaches people how to dissociate from their body, restrict their nutrition, and regulate their feelings of self-worth through the shape of their body. Believe it or not, dieting is also a set up for mindless eating. When people feel deprived, they crave the forbidden food, and when they finally eat it, they are much more likely to overeat.

Students and Dieting

For students, there is another significant drawback to fad dieting. Purposefully restricting calories can actually interfere with achieving academic goals. Repeatedly, dieting has been shown to negatively affect cognitive performance and inhibit memory (Jones and Rogers 2003; McFarlane, Polivy, and McCabe 1999). This means that dieters often find it harder to concentrate, recall facts, and remember what they've read. So, right before a big history final may be the worst time for students to cut carbohydrates or drastically lower the fat in their diet.

There are two theories proposed to explain why it's harder for dieters to think clearly. One theory is based on the effect of food deprivation. Basically, reducing calorie intake and the availability of glucose often leads to a reduction in energy. When energy is low, the brain and body overall slow down and work less efficiently. The brain is deprived of the energy it needs to work at full capacity.

Yet, there has been some evidence to disprove this theory. When subjects are deprived of food, but not "dieting" per se, their cognitive performance isn't as affected. This suggests that not only the physical, but also the psychological effects of food deprivation are involved. For example, researchers gave dieters a chocolate bar to see if it would improve their cognitive performance on memory tests. Many of the dieters reported feeling so guilty about eating the chocolate that they couldn't think about anything else. Two-thirds of the dieters even admitted they had thought about hiding or disposing of the chocolate rather than eating it (Jones and Rogers 2003).

This gives a lot of credence to the second theory, which has nothing to do with the metabolic changes from calories or energy. Some people, when they are hungry, can't think about anything else besides food. The mind becomes preoccupied with thoughts about food, how to manage hunger, weight, and planning out future meals. This doesn't leave much room for math, history, and term papers.

Ending the Battle

Undergraduate and graduate students are alarmed by the prevalence of fad diets, the thin ideal, and unhealthy food options and are quite ready to end the fighting. For this reason, college students are becoming better informed, more savvy, and more discerning food consumers. Move over mystery meat and corn casserole surprise, make room for a new group of students who demand a healthier student body—literally. They want to be at peace with themselves so they can take full advantage of all there is to offer socially and academically in college.

Why Eating More Mindfully Is Important

The benefits of eating mindfully are self-evident. Mindful eating is associated with living a healthier, longer life. Mindful eating can help you avoid some of the well-documented short- and long-term consequences of overeating, such as high blood pressure, cancer, diabetes, high cholesterol, hypertension, and coronary heart disease. Obesity and smoking are two health problems that are the leading causes of death right now.

Eating mindfully also helps to ensure that you get adequate nutrition. Foods containing the correct combination of vitamins and minerals give you enough energy to complete all of your responsibilities. A balanced diet does wonders for your health, not only in the present but for the rest of your life.

Another bonus of eating mindfully is that it improves self-esteem, while mindless eating, with the inevitable weight issues, significantly infringes upon self-confidence. Students who have become overweight, or feel they are headed in that direction, are afraid of ridicule, being turned down by potential dating partners or at the very least of being discounted by their peers. We live in a society in which there is an enormous amount of pressure to be thin and to have a flawless body. It is the fear of being judged for even the slightest gain in weight that sets many students on an unhealthy course.

Mindfulness

Just because you decide to eat more mindfully, doesn't mean you necessarily know how to get the ball rolling. In my opinion, the first step to changing your eating habits is to develop a new mindfulness, or self-awareness.

The best way to understand mindfulness is to experience it. As you read this text, you are cultivating a mindful state or a conscious "awareness." All the clutter has been cleared out of your head and you devote your full attention to the text. There may well be a hundred different places where your attention could be focused, but at this very moment you are blocking it out so that your full attention is focused right here, right now.

However, if your awareness is "divided," perhaps you are reading the present text while also thinking about midterms or about what to wear tomorrow, this is a case of mindless reading. In order to learn the true motivation for your actions, your attention must be fully focused on those thoughts and feelings that are connected to each and every action in daily life.

Zoned In and Zoned Out

Student life is rich with mindful and mindless moments. In each moment, mindfulness is either turned on or off—a mindful or a mindless state. For example, some days you may attend class, both physically and mentally. You show up on time and are actively involved in the class discussion. On other days, when the room is too stuffy and the professor is dry as a bone, you zone out. Although your body is sitting upright in the chair and your eyes are open, it's all an illusion. Your brain and body can be in two completely different places at once; this is a state of mindlessness.

When you become aware that you have missed a few crucial moments of the lecture, it's no problem. You become mindful again by listening to what the professor is saying and feeling your legs against the cool, uncomfortable desk chair. Your body and mind are again both sitting in a classroom.

In this example, you have chosen to bring your awareness back to the task at hand. At other times, there are external forces that make us mindful, such as a bell ringing or the teacher calling out your name. The world often begs you to be mindful and insists that your mental presence is sorely missed.

Missing a few minutes of class isn't the end of the world. But, in extreme cases, mindless behavior can have major consequences. For example, one of my clients, a junior in college, began therapy after a semester studying abroad in London. In England, she made a shopping date with one of her American friends who was also studying abroad. They agreed to meet at a designated spot on Oxford Street. When she saw her friend, she motioned for her to cross over to her side of the street. The friend turned her head to the left, stepped out into the street and walked right into a speeding car (in England traffic goes on the left rather than the right side of the road). In London, instructions to "look right" or "look left" are written on the street at street crossings to remind people to be alert. It is easy to imagine how traumatizing it was to witness such a simple act of mindless behavior with such devastating consequences.

The Origins of Mindfulness

Ancient civilizations knew how important it was to have a clear and present mind. These classic mindfulness meditation techniques are still popular today and are gaining renewed respect in many scientific communities for their unique healing qualities. Yes, being mindful is actually therapeutic. It is so psychologically beneficial that mindfulness skills help people cope with everyday stressors and have been incorporated into treatments for a wide variety of problems such as everyday stress, AIDS, cancer, depression, and chronic pain (Baer 2003).

Mindfulness and College Students

Therapists have begun integrating and adapting meditation and mindfulness practices to fit the modern college student's life. For example, research shows that mindfulness can successfully help medical students cope with stress (Rosenzweig, Reibel, Greeson, Brainard, and Hojat 2003; Shapiro, Schwartz, and Bonner 1998). After just a few weeks of mindfulness training, there was a significant reduction in negative mood amongst stressed out medical students. In general, meditation and relaxation skills can help students cope with the day to day demands of college life (Deckro, Ballinger, Hoyt, Wilcher, Dusek, Myers, Greensberg, Rosenthal, and Benson 2002). Mindfulness is also part of treatments used to assist people in gaining control over their eating habits (Baer 2003; Kristeller and Hallett 1999; Safer, Telch, and Agras 2001, Wisniewski and Kelly 2003). Therapists are currently blending mindfulness with many traditional psychological treatments.

How Does Mindfulness Work?

Mindfulness works on two levels. It can have a positive effect on the body and thoughts. Some studies show that when people are mindful, they experience an increase in EEG alpha brain waves associated with a state of relaxation (Baer 2003). As brain rhythms slow, natural pain killers and endorphins are released. Also, when the body becomes more relaxed, the heart rate, levels of stress hormones, and respiration rate all decrease and the body moves into a relaxed state. These physiological changes make a person better able to cope with stress and the negative emotions that accompany problems. When a person is calm, it is much easier to focus and come up with healthy coping strategies rather than gravitating toward old unhealthy patterns. Other benefits include strengthening the immune system and increasing activity in the part of the brain that manages emotion (Davidson et al. 2003).

Mindfulness can also change the way people think. This is the main benefit of being mindful. When a person is aware and present, he or she makes better decisions rather than falling into habitual routines. For example, anxiety about a problem will lead to a feeling of stress. This panic state can develop that prevents rational thought patterns from taking place, such as checking through all of the available options. Later, when a feeling of calm has been achieved, the individual may think "hmm, why didn't I think to do x, y, or z. . . ." The stress had set in and blocked clear, productive thinking.

Eating Mindfully: Putting Your Mind Where Your Mouth Is

So, how do you become more aware and in turn gain more control over feeding your appetite? Eating mindfully means simply paying attention with an open, nonjudgmental mind to what and how you eat. Mindful eaters are just more aware of what they feel and think as they eat. As closer attention is paid to what you put in your mouth, much better choices begin to be made. It's like paying attention to how much money you spend. If you just buy on a whim, you end up overspending on junk that it is clear later is neither needed nor wanted. Alternatively, you might become so restrictive that you miss out on an essential item. However, if you keep track of your budget, it is possible to have the best of both worlds. Eating mindfully is very similar: You should not overly restrict yourself, but neither should you respond to every impulse to eat.

The first step to being more mindful is to open up your awareness level, and the next chapter discusses how this can take place.

> ***Introduction: Mindful Eating 101:*** Direct your attention to any inner food fights. What are your weapons of choice? Fad diets? Scathing words about your body? Guilt? It's essential to identify the emotional effects of the ongoing battle. Is it overpowering? Embarrassing? Painful? Tiring? It's important for you to bear in mind any feelings you may have regarding current food battles. Imagine what it would feel like to end mindless eating and live at peace with your body.

Part One

Mindless Eating in College

Chapter 1

Sex, Drugs, and Rocky Road Ice Cream

Opening Up Awareness

"I despise William Dreyer," lamented Jane, a college student and one of my psychotherapy clients. With a scowl, she said, "William is responsible for making my life miserable. Well... William, economics class, and my psycho roommate, in that order." She crossed her arms and slumped down in the office chair. Jane had been my client at a college counseling center for about three months. I wracked my brain for a moment and silently reviewed in my head all the stories she had told me about her friends, enemies, and ex-lovers. No William came to mind.

Who is William Dreyer, I asked?

Jane explained that this mystery man first became the object of her hatred while she was writing a paper for her business economics class on entrepreneurs. "William Dreyer is the coinventor of Rocky Road ice cream," she explained in an exasperated tone. Rocky Road Ice Cream was invented by Dreyer, an ice cream maker and Joseph Edy, a candy maker around 1929. Mr. Dreyer used his wife's sewing shears to cut up the marshmallows and then sprinkled in some of Edy's candy, so the story goes. The partners named it Rocky Road in honor of the Great Depression. They wanted to give people something to smile about during such a rough time in the world.

"Sure, William wanted to make people 'happy' but did he realize that he would be creating rocky road-aholics" she pondered out loud?

"I wouldn't have gained the freshman thirty if it hadn't been for him!" Jane said. "They have gallons, no . . . vats of Rocky Road Ice cream in the cafeteria dining hall. I forbid myself to even look at it but it's like a Pavlovian response. I see it and start salivating. Literally, I want to swan dive tongue first into the ten-gallon tub of ice cream filled with candy bits, chopped nuts, and gooey marshmallows. I mindlessly eat away. One bowl turns into two before I even know it. I sit in class and suddenly realize that I am daydreaming about ice cream. If I eat too much, the guilt is unbearable. I feel so full and fat. My evening is destroyed. Who can study when you have a Rocky Road hangover?"

Unfortunately, Jane's description of mindlessly overeating Rocky Road was familiar to me. She was not the only student I worked with who felt sucked into the cafeteria vortex. So many students struggle with this cycle of mindless overeating and then feeling guilty.

As she described her issue, I also had a sinking feeling deep in my gut. The legend of the freshman fifteen had struck again. The number had somehow jumped from the freshman fifteen to the freshman thirty almost overnight. In the three months I had known her, Jane didn't visibly appear to have gained any weight. She wore the same pair of faded, low rise jeans every other week. It was more likely her fear of weight gain that had gotten heavier and harder to deal with.

The Mindless Eating Cycle

Jane was not *aware* of what was truly causing the mindless eating issue. She thought the ice cream was the problem, but it wasn't always the real issue. Sometimes Jane just misjudging her hunger by misreading her body's cues. But, other times, she was stuck in what I call the "mindless eating cycle." The cycle began like this. When she got a grade on a paper that fell below her expectations, she took it pretty hard. Jane had such high expectations of herself. She was a perfectionist, which made her constantly feel below par. These snags in her self-esteem caused anxiety. Often, she didn't know to manage the negative feelings. When

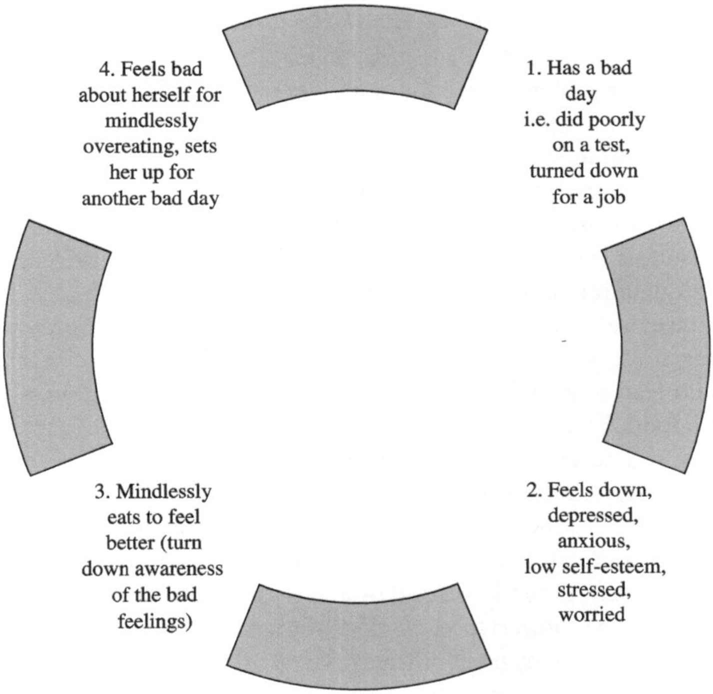

Figure 1.1 The Mindless Eating Cycle.

the "I can't do anything right feeling" returned, she sought out a quick pick-me-up. Jane got into the habit of mindlessly eating ice cream. There was a lot of the ice cream available and she knew it made her feel better. The Rocky Road ice cream distracted her from her worries and it tasted divine. But, after she'd eaten it, she'd experienced guilt and her stomach would feel very uncomfortable. This discomfort led her to feel "anxious, fat, and mad" at herself for mindlessly overeating yet again. The cycle would begin once more.

Sex, Drugs, and Rocky Road Ice Cream

When we are disappointed in ourselves or feel inadequate, we must find ways to cope with it to restore a sense of well-being. We look for something that makes us feel "okay" again. Food, sex, or other substances are high on the list of things people use to temporarily soothe their pain, boredom or stress. For college students, all of these substances are so readily accessible. Notice that food, sex, and alcohol in moderation and in healthy, legal contexts, can be enjoyable. But, in the extreme, or when they aren't kept in check, they are unhealthy dangerous, even deadly. Acting on every impulse for sex, for example, could lead to a nightmare of consequences. The same thing occurs with food. Every urge to eat is not about being hungry. So, acting on every urge to eat is not always healthy.

Sure, it's totally normal to seek out a little chocolate, ice cream, or other comfort food. We all do it. Every now and then we crave a snack that pleases the tongue and is guaranteed to make us feel good. But, when we turn to food over and over again to numb out or to get that little high, the comfort food can turn from the comfort to the problem.

Looking in my psychotherapy crystal ball, I would have predicted several things for Jane if she continued this mindless eating pattern and did not deal with her self-esteem issues, the real issue at hand. Today, she blamed poor Mr. Dreyer whose only crime was inventing delicious ice cream. By tomorrow, she was likely to be angry at Mr. Strauss, the inventor of blue jeans. Without getting a handle on the food issue, I feared she would plunge into fad dieting. Since, 35 percent of "typical dieters" progress to more problematic eating habits, the Rocky Road mindless eating had the potential to evolve into a more serious eating concern (Shisslak, Crago, and Estes 1995).

Instead, Jane created a very different future. She transformed from the "freshman thirty" phobic to someone who accepted herself and quit letting her perfectionism stand in the way. When the emotional handicap melted away, it left in its place a woman who loved ice cream unconditionally, accepted her body, and didn't let her self-esteem cripple her. Here is how she did it.

Awareness

In a nutshell, Jane's first step to overcoming her eating issues was through developing a new awareness. She paid close attention to her behavior to find out what was really driving the "mindless eating cycle." There was a predictable pattern. When Jane had a bad day or made a mistake, she craved the ice cream. Cutting the ice cream out of Jane's diet wasn't necessary. To end the "cycle," she had to find other ways to manage her stress, pay extremely close attention to her hunger, and get out of the habit of turning to food to feel better quickly. When she pushed the mindless eating issues of ice cream aside, she realize that there were lots of places in her life that she felt were not good enough. She became aware that feeling inadequate underscored a lot of her unhealthy, mindless eating behaviors. Then, she used skills in this book to help her become a more mindful eater.

Opening Up Awareness

Although there are many avenues to opening up one's awareness, when it comes to getting control over mindless eating habits, there are two highlighted in this chapter: (1) focusing on the issue rather than pushing it away, and (2) breaking out of mindless routines. Without getting a handle on these two topics, it's unlikely that you would become conscious of what would be helpful to change. It's like catching a spelling mistake that was missed the first time a paper was proofread. Once the error has been caught, it's impossible to turn a blind eye to it or forget that it's there. But, if the error isn't even seen, the mistake can't be corrected.

What Is Awareness?

We live in a culture that pushes us to move faster and faster. PDAs, cell phones, modems, teleconferencing are just a few of the technological advances we use in our everyday lives. Yet, they are also evidence that our culture is pushing us into fast forward mode. It's a speed that is sometimes hard to keep up with it. The pace of our world falls in line with the philosophy of people movers (moving walkways) you see at airports. They imply that walking isn't good enough—walk at double speed, move faster. Staying in sync with this kind of pace prevents us from paying attention to what is going on in the moment. We are so quickly moving on to the next task that we aren't focused on what is taking place in that very second. When we aren't living in the moment it leaves little time to understand the feelings and thoughts that motivate us to do what we do.

We just try to keep up, move faster, and often can barely keep up with the pace. We end up simply going through the motions to get by. Imagine, for example, a woman who is trying to fit in all of her prerequisite classes in order to graduate with a history major in four years. She is also working twenty hours a week to pay for college and is constantly worried about how to get research assistantships. The assistantships are necessary resume builders so that she can be competitive enough to get a job. Does she ever really slow down to ask herself whether she is enjoying this? Is this degree really what she wants or is it just what her parents expect of her? Where is her life going? Is she happy? No, she doesn't stop to ask herself these questions because she is too busy keeping up with the demands of the outside world. On top of meeting the expectations of the academic world and her parents, her own desire for success pushes her to move at double speed. Like this woman, we often believe we have little time to slow down and think about our feelings. In addition to being maxed out on time, sometimes we just aren't ready to face what's going on inside.

"I'll Worry About That Tomorrow" Syndrome

Throughout the classic 1930s movie *Gone with the Wind*, which takes place during the Civil War, Scarlett O'Hara, the fiery Southern heroine, shares with us her philosophy on dealing with life's woes: "I can't worry about that now, I'll think about that tomorrow." Over and over again, she determines that she just can't handle things in the moment.

She shoves all her painful thoughts, including the loss of her love, Rhett Butler, right out of her head. Scarlett keeps feelings like guilt, regret, jealousy, and loss below her awareness radar.

We get the "I'll worry about that tomorrow" syndrome with so many issues in life. Consciously and unconsciously we push painful and uncomfortable things to the back of the mind, down deep into the crevices. The mind attempts to shield us from pain by shoving hurtful things to the back of the brain. It's like putting a painful break-up letter from an ex in the very back corner of the closet: it is a case of hoping that out of sight is out of mind. But, the letter is there and it can be bothersome when something makes one remember it.

In part, pushing things out of our minds is an adaptive response. If we dwelled all day long on hurtful things, our worlds would come to an abrupt halt. We couldn't function. Putting it aside helps us cope with the pain. Yet, if you don't ever come back to it and deal with the problem it can pop up when you least expect it. In the end, putting her emotional baggage aside didn't even work for Scarlett in *Gone with the Wind.* Eventually, she loses her husband Rhett, and it doesn't dawn on her until after he leaves her to really stop and consider her true feelings for him: She is in love with him.

While shielding awareness of problems may temporarily make us feel better, ignoring problems only makes it more difficult to find true resolution. A small problem becomes overwhelming. Let's take the example of a term paper that was due in six weeks and you put off working on it until two days before it was due. Meanwhile, every book in the library on the subject has been checked out. You are in big trouble because you may fail the class if the paper isn't turned in on time.

When there is an issue that you don't want to face, this is when you are likely to have the hardest time standing still, or being mindful. You may find yourself signing up for more school activities and social clubs. Your friends notice that you are busier than ever and don't have time to talk. Sometimes the busyness is a way of keeping away the real issue at a "safe" distance. If you stop and be still for too long, discomfort could arise and then you'd really have to think about the whys and wherefores. With mindless eating issues, you can find a million things to keep yourself so busy that you don't have time to focus on the root of the problem.

Fighting off the issue is sometimes worse than the actual problem. For example, one of my clients was determined to hide her overeating problem. To protect her secret from her roommates, she got up at 4:30 A.M. every single day to eat. For an hour, she would eat a bagel or two, candy, left over pizza, anything that she could get her hands on. She wanted to have the house to herself to eat in private. Getting up early shielded her secret and her embarrassment, but getting up that early each day left her sleep deprived, so, she slept through some of her classes. Not only did she have an eating problem, but it now grew into an academic problem. Therefore, an important aspect of being *aware* is about really directing your attention to the mindless eating issues rather than pushing them out of your head or below your conscious awareness.

The Trance of Eating: Eating Without Awareness

Eating is such a simple act that we often downshift into a gear of low awareness while we eat. Unless you actively decide to pay attention, you don't really have to think much about eating—just pick up the fork and eat. Mentally, you don't have to be very present. Sometimes you may feel that your mind has completely checked out. "I can't stop eating this piece of cake, my body has a mind of it's own!"

Because we eat at least three times a day, most of us have preferred eating habits and daily food rituals. Maybe you eat lunch at noon every day. Maybe you tend to buy the same foods from week to week. Is Monday night always pasta and meatballs? Location can also get repetitive: you may eat pizza in front of the TV, prefer to hang out at a particular dining hall, or eat at the same handful of restaurants on Friday nights. Maybe you ask for the same kind of birthday cake each year—yellow cake with pineapple filling from a special bakery.

The bottom line is that people are often predictable about their eating preferences and habits.

These "habits" get people stuck. You tend to automatically go back to old behaviors when you aren't consciously thinking about your actions. Even when you want to change something, you have to force yourself not to revert back to your previous ways. It's similar to changing an e-mail password. If you use e-mail daily, you type in your password with little to no thought. When the password is changed, you're likely to continue to type in the old one for awhile, until you actively stop yourself, pay attention to what you are doing, and mindfully type in the new password. You have to break out of the programmed autopilot. So, it's easy to see why it so tough to change everyday, routine eating habits.

Ups and Downs of Mindless Routines

The benefit of forming routines is that they are predictable. You don't have to think about what to eat, and the routines provide structure to the day. Adam goes to the same bagel shop every day before work and orders the same thing—a bagel and a medium coffee. He knows what he is having for breakfast and how much it will cost. This type of routine saves time because planning meals is time consuming. Perhaps it would take him an extra half an hour to make himself pancakes. Maybe he forgot to buy milk at the supermarket and it is inconvenient to run to the store to pick up a quart of milk for cereal. The effortlessness of stopping at the bagel shop every day is extremely attractive.

Routines, as attractive as they seem, diminish your sense of awareness. As you go through the motions of the day, you may not even remember individual actions. How many times have you thought, "Did I eat lunch?" You know that you always eat a Hot Pocket at noon between chemistry and environmental science classes, and now it is one o'clock and there is no Hot Pocket in your backpack. You must have glossed over it or rushed through it. It might be hard to change this habit of eating a Hot Pocket on the run as you do every single day like clockwork. It happens even if you aren't conscious of doing it.

When food becomes a routine way of coping with daily problems, a serious issue has developed. If you feel bad, you immediately (and maybe even unconsciously) reach out and shove food into our mouth. Or, perhaps in times of intense stress, you automatically stop eating even when you are hungry. In either scenario, mindless eaters automatically turn toward or away from food. Thus, it is a slippery slope into serious eating problems that can begin when a mindless eater stops eating lunch during the stress of finals and forgets to start eating lunch again after finals are finished.

Mindless Food Rules

"I can't eat red meat more than once a day." "Chocolate is a no-no." "I can have one cookie but not two." These are some classic examples of self-imposed food rules. Food rules reduce awareness and allow the brain to grow lazy. Sometimes individuals seek out food rules because it means not having to think very hard. If there is a guideline set, no decision has to be made.

Following food rules blindly is a problem because the rules often don't take into account the situation or the circumstance. For example, your food rule instructs you not to eat cake. But, it is your birthday and your boyfriend has made you a special chocolate cake from scratch. What are you to do?

"Don't Eat the French Fries"

A study of college students' food journals reveals that, like the rest of the population, students lean a lot on food rules (Counihan 1992). They too make long mental lists of "good" or "bad" foods. What's intriguing about food rules is that they can be wildly conflicting and illogical. Eating ice cream is an "okay" dairy food but Swiss cheese is totally taboo and "bad." How does that make sense? When you ask people to explain the origin of their food rules they often point to a variety of unscientific sources. Sometimes the rules are based on a magazine article, while at other times, the rule was created from a "fact" someone told them about peanut butter.

Mindfulness of Food Rules

Being mindful of these rules means bringing the rules and assumptions to the very surface of our brain and challenging them. Why is chocolate a "bad" food? Is it really a "horrible" thing to eat after nine if I'm really hungry? Why don't I trust my body to tell me when to start and stop eating? It's not a question of getting rid of the rules or throwing them out. But it is important to begin to ask yourself how the rules got there in the first place and what purpose they serve. Instead of food rules, mindful eaters depend on "being in the moment."

Being in the Moment

Mindful eaters try to "be in the moment." As trite and impossible as it sounds, *being in the moment* means not thinking about the past or the future but just being aware of what is going on in that very moment. This means, in the case of food, focusing only on what is being eaten at the moment it is being eaten. Most of us use hindsight to understand why we did something. After eating a piece of cheesecake, you may say, "Why did I eat that entire piece? I wasn't even hungry?" Then, you may think back and explore the possible reasons for the mindless eating. Perhaps you overate because you hadn't had cheesecake in a while. But, it's too late to really be sure, because the event is over, the cheesecake has been eaten.

When you are in the moment, you evaluate your motivation and sensations as they are happening—such as asking why you are eating this particular food at this particular moment. What am I feeling as I eat this cheesecake? How does it taste? Do I really like it? Am I really hungry? When these questions are asked at this point in the proceedings, you can understand your motivation and still have the option of making a choice. Then it is possible to decide whether you are really enjoying the food, eating it mindfully, and will keep eating it. Or, there's the option of noting that you aren't really hungry, that although the food was good, to continue eating it will lead to some regret for eating mindlessly. There is still a choice. It may or may not change the action, but it gives you the power and control to make a conscious decision.

Give Mindful Eating a Try!

We have all eaten an entire plate of food and not tasted one single bite. It is essential to bring all of your senses to the dinner table. Identify the taste—salty, sour, sweet, bitter, unami—from the Japanese). Eat with an open, conscious awareness. Instead of shovel, scoop, and insert, try look, taste, and savor.

For a brief "taste" of eating mindfully, try the following exercise. Let's use the example of snacking on popcorn. To begin, observe the shape and color of each popped kernel. Notice the variations in the shape and the white and brown color. Feel the texture. Notice the taste of salt. Then, listen to the crunch of each bite and the noise made by chewing. Feel the rough texture as the popcorn is ground between the teeth, and the sensation as it slides down the throat. Each bite should be experienced from start to finish. Be fully aware of every movement, swallow, aroma, and feeling. This is the first minilesson in mindful eating. Try it out at the next meal.

Putting Your Mind in the Driver's Seat: Seven Ways to Be More Mindfully Aware

Here is a summary of seven elements that can result in increased mindfulness. They are key points to opening up awareness. This list includes: *pure awareness, observing, shifting out of "autopilot," looking at the gray areas, being in the moment, nonjudgment, and acceptance* (Baer 2003; Kabat-Zinn 1990; Linehan 1993; Zindel, Williams, and Teasdale 2001). Throughout this book, each section describes how these seven skills can be used to improve body image, body language, relationships, and self-esteem.

Figure 1.2 Seven Keys to Mindful Eating

1. **Awareness involves using the senses:** Each of the senses collects information about the world and detects changes within the body. The external senses are hearing, sight, taste, touch, and smell. Feeling pain, balance, energy, thirst, and hunger are internal senses. They give information about the body and its needs. For example, the sensation of hunger alerts you to the need for food. Feeling pain lets you know that a wound exists and must be attended to. When you pay close attention to all of these sensations, you are gathering information about how to accurately feed your hunger.
2. **Observing involves simply being watchful of your thoughts, behavior, and feelings without trying to alter them in any way:** Nothing has to be done or changed. Observing involves being an *impartial witness or observer* to your thoughts and feelings. An impartial witness would step aside and gently point out each time a negative thought was trying to influence a decision about what to eat. It would say, "Look, it is happening again. You just had a thought about the freshman fifteen and now you are anxious about your weight." Watching feelings and labeling thoughts provides more control.
3. **Shifting out of autopilot involves getting out of the routines that allow you to go through the motions with very little thought:** Daily activities like brushing your teeth, walking to class, and eating are so routine that you could do them in your sleep. You also don't have to think very hard to eat—you just do it. When eating takes place out of mindless habit without real thought being involved, it is called "eating on autopilot" (e.g., picking at a bread basket at a restaurant). Real awareness involves taking note of each action—thinking about picking up a spoon; being conscious of the taste and warmth of each spoonful of chicken noodle soup.
4. **Looking at the gray areas involves moving away from extremes and finding a balanced, middle ground:** Yes or no, good or bad, the fact is that few things in life are completely wrong or absolutely wonderful. Looking at the gray areas is about gaining

a balance between black and white extremes, or all or nothing categories. In regard to eating, it involves finding a moderate balance between eating too much and too little. And it is also above all about developing flexibility and losing the rigid rules laid out by diets.

5. **Being in the moment involves paying attention to an experience that is happening in this very moment rather than dwelling on the past or hurrying into the future:** A college lifestyle is anything but in the here and now: no sleep, late night parties, three papers due on one day. Living in the moment means making eating a priority rather than eating on the run, skipping a meal, or multitasking during a meal. It involves sitting down and eating without being in a hurry. The eater's focus is on the food which means being present mentally and physically during the meal.
6. **Being nonjudgmental means noticing the judgmental and critical thoughts used to label experience as good or bad. Instead, be more compassionate:** Statements that include the shoulds, shouldn'ts, and other judgmental language really shut down awareness. We shrink away from critical comments. Compassionate self-talk involves gentle and truthful self-statements. A nonjudgmental attitude helps you to make better food choices. You can then decide what to eat based on what is appropriate rather than trying to cope with the shame produced by critical thoughts.
7. **Acceptance involves coming to terms with things as they really are versus how we wish they would be:** Acceptance is having the attitude of "it is what it is" and "I am who I am" without trying to change it. It's like the attitude most of us adopt toward our height or shoe size. Even if you'd like to be taller or have smaller feet, eventually you accept your size. Not accepting yourself, or having unrealistic expectations keeps people very stuck in a cycle of feeling bad about themselves. Being critical often doesn't motivate positive, lasting change. Acceptance involves building a stronger foundation to build yourself up on.

Chapter 1, Mindful Eating 101: Listen closely to what your body is telling you is essential. Intimately get to know your hunger. Observe nonjudgmentally the thoughts and feelings that kick-start your appetite. Be really aware of what starts and stops you from eating.

Chapter 2

Mindless Eating vs. Mindful Eating

Confessions of a Dieter

At lunch today, I looked down at my cafeteria tray. My green beans were swimming around in what seemed to be an entire stick of butter. The water and butter had made war and separated into little globs at either end of the bowl. I scooped out the beans to save them from drowning in the buttery soup. I hoped to remove any trace of fat by blotting them with the napkins I grabbed from the table dispenser.

Here is what dieting has taught me to do. Before I eat anything, I cut it open, tear off the cheese and slice apart meat to eliminate any trace of fat. I push aside pats of butter, scrap off excess BBQ sauce, shove off traces of maple syrup from pancakes and blot away extra oil off the top of pizza. I have scooted, picked, sliced, trimmed, and daintily "eaten like a bird." Other times, I use my fingers to scrap, tear, or throw food off my plate.

It was the "the green bean" incident that first made me truly mindful of my bizarre relationship with dieting. Food and green beans are meant to be savored and have great nutritional qualities and I took away these attributes. I decided at that moment to be more attentive to my behavior and start making some healthy changes. Food is to be enjoyed not picked apart.

Is this woman's eating behavior cause for serious alarm? Or, can it be passed off as casual dieting? Mindless eaters often start out as dieters. They turn to fad dieting hoping that it will fix their mindless eating issues. However, dieters are very different from mindful eaters. This chapter helps distinguish between the behaviors and attitudes of dieters, mindful, and mindless eaters. It breaks down mindless eaters even further into the categories of overeaters, undereaters, and chaotic eaters.

The Diet Club

Thankfully, the majority of us do not suffer from serious eating problems. However, it may *feel* as though everyone has food issues because dieting and food anxiety is such a prevalent part of Western culture. Dieting is often the first place people turn to for help when trying to break their mindless eating habits. In an effort to gain control over their mindless eating, Americans spend approximately fifty billon dollars annually on diet products.

So many people worry about their mindless eating habits that deciding to go on a diet can feel a little like joining a very large social club, fraternity, or sorority. Anyone can join and members can come and go as they please. In fact, members can quit and rejoin the diet club every day if they wish. Eighty percent of students admit that they have tried dieting to lose weight and 32 percent had dieted six or more times (Clayton et al. 1997). Dieters invite roommates, friends, and family to join the "club" with them. They entice people to join by preying on the universal wish to be more attractive. "Hey, I'm trying this new diet.... Wanna give it a try? I lost weight and so can you." You can almost feel the adrenaline rush starting to pulse through your veins with the very thought of being thinner. Who wouldn't want to join in?

Once a would-be dieter has signed up for this club, dieters seem to follow unwritten rules of social etiquette. Club members speak in the universal fad diet lingo of self-judgment, self–dislike, and fear. Eating distress and body loathing has led millions to consider joining this so-called club of chronic dieters. According to one statistic from the National Eating Disorders Association, approximately 45 percent of American women and 25 percent of men are on a diet every day. Pretty scary. Not only is dieting considered a "normal" behavior it is at times even admired and taught in books and magazines. We honor people for dieting through our actions and comments like "Wow, you really have a lot of willpower sticking to that diet."

Is Dieting Mindful?

Fad dieting is not a mindful behavior. It doesn't fit the bill for several reasons. First, reading fad diet books can make mindless eating worse. The more you know about carbohydrates and fats, the more dependent you are on nutrition labels, which turns you away from your internal awareness or paying attention to your own stomach. We've all witnessed people who happily pick up a single serving snack, turn over the package, scan the nutrition label, and put it back with utter dismay. Fad diet books often teach consumers what to fear on nutrition labels rather than showing them how to use the information as a positive, helpful tool.

Diets can be very judgmental. Take, for example, magazine articles like "Ten Foods You Should Never Eat." In an article like this, a variety of foods are judged to be "bad." The tone of the article implies that the person who would even consider eating these taboo foods is not wise.

It's not rocket science that we should eat when we are hungry and stop eating when we are full. However, when we are dieting, we start to forget what those experiences feel like. Hunger becomes a muddled, confusing sensation. If you ignore your stomach, after a while your body isn't going to bother telling you when it is hungry. It already knows you won't answer.

Mindful eating doesn't make you any promises like diets do. It's not short-term. It is intended to be a plan you can live with forever. You may or may not lose weight. There aren't any firm or steadfast rules. No foods are cut out or off limits. You aim for moderation and balance in all your food choices. You have a healthy awareness of what you eat.

Range of Aware and Unaware Eating

The range of eating awareness is vast. The level of awareness can be a ten or a zero depending on the individual's frame of mind. A ten would be hypervigilant, overly alert, and watchful of every aspect of eating, counting each calorie. A five may be very conscious of every single bite, aware, and notice the taste and aroma of each morsel (e.g., "Wow, this soup is really salty" or "Mmm, this yogurt is so creamy and fluffy"). On the other end of the spectrum, a one may be in a zombie state, chomping mindlessly away at a big tub of popcorn and getting to the bottom of the bowl without even realizing that popcorn had been eaten.

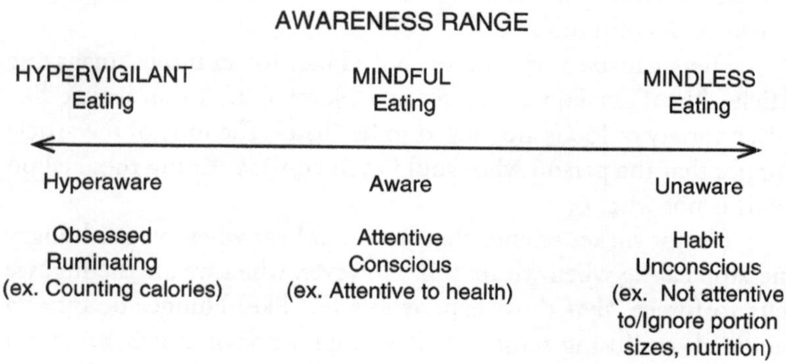

Figure 2.1 Mindful Eating: The Range of Awareness

What Is Mindful Eating?

"I am aware of what I eat. My health, nutrition, self-esteem, and overall well-being are important to me."

Mindful Awareness

My friend told me that she admired my attitude about eating and that I was her role model. Me? A role model? I took for granted that I don't worry much about food. Instead, I am just very "aware" of what I eat.

I compare how I eat to my sleeping habits. If I don't get the "right" or healthy amount of sleep, I'm a mess. Sometimes on Saturday mornings I oversleep and on nights I'm cramming for a test, I don't get a wink. The rest of the time, I shoot for a solid seven hours. It's the same thing with food. Every now and then I splurge because I really, really love chocolate cake. And sometimes, I miss a meal because I'm so busy. For the most part, I just try to be mindful or aware about what I eat and how much I exercise. I don't know how many calories are in a cookie, but I know they taste good and too many will make me feel sick. I don't eat every single thing I want. That wouldn't be healthy either.

Mindful Eating

Being as Aware of Why You Eat as What You Eat

Mindful eaters consciously think about what they eat. They keep close tabs on the physical, social, and emotional motivation underlying their eating. They eat a balanced and varied menu of foods based on the needs of their own body. Their attitude is aware, flexible, and nonjudgmental.

Notice that a mindful eater doesn't eat every single thing he or she wants. For example, a person standing in front of a bakery window could pick many treats she would want. However, eating four or five desserts would make her sick to her stomach. Sometimes we think that the ability to "eat anything you want" is a sign of health. If we really ate everything we desired, we'd probably all be eating chocolate bonbons 24/7.

A mindful eater pays attention to the connection between how well the body functions and getting the proper amount of vitamins and minerals. The body sends very subtle cues when it is depleted of certain nutrients. We often pass off as stress such symptoms as feeling run down when it could be an imbalance caused by a lack of healthy foods. For example, you might be more likely to feel tired when you don't have enough iron in your system. Or, frequent colds may be related to a lack of vitamin C.

The National Eating Disorder Association offers a word of wisdom on their Web site. This organization advises that healthy individuals *"EAT WHAT YOU WANT — When you are truly hungry. Stop when you are full."* A person who can do this trusts their body to know when to start and stop eating. This advice fits well with the definition of a mindful eater.

Mindful Eating

> *As I am walking to class, I notice that I am spending the entire trip pondering what I am going to eat for lunch. Hmm. I must be pretty hungry to give it this much thought. I'm not starving but I need more than a quick snack. Should I have a fajita wrap? No, the cafeteria always drowns it with way too much dressing and it is soggy and sloppy. Maybe I can leave off the dressing? A salad? I don't think so, I'll be starving by dinner. A special healthy cuisine entree? No, it's way too expensive for my student's work study salary and I don't have time for that. I just don't know what to eat. Wow, I'm thinking really hard about this. I'm surprised how difficult it is to just pick something. That thought just made me kind of annoyed. Ugh oh, when I'm annoyed I tend to choose anything just to get it over with. It's okay. I tend to panic when you are feeling this rushed. I need to choose something filling with some protein. If I order the nachos, it will be quick but I'd be setting myself up. I almost always mindlessly eat the nachos and cheese. I love the chicken salad sandwich—ah, that is just right. It tastes good and will keep me satisfied until this evening.*

This is an example of a student in the midst of mindfully choosing her lunch. She keeps track of the running dialogue going on her in her head. She labels her feeling—she's annoyed. Identifying this feeling and the potential consequences of letting that emotion be in control helps her sidestep mindless eating. She thinks through all of the cafeteria's options carefully.

Mindful eating involves the following elements:

- Flexibility (no food is banned or cut out of a diet).
- All foods are eaten mindfully and in moderation (desserts, fruits, vegetables, grains, proteins, etc.).
- Really taste food and each bite.
- Mindful eaters don't stress out too much about what they eat. However, if they do feel anxious when thinking about calories, they acknowledge it and work through it.
- Awareness of nutrition. The focus is on health not dieting.
- Food is considered a fuel not the enemy.
- Paying attention to the process of eating (picking up the fork, using it to put a mouthful of food in one's mouth).
- Using all of the senses: smell, taste, touch, and inhaling the aroma.
- Being fully in the moment while eating. Bringing one's attention back to eating when the mind wanders.
- Listening to the body. Eating when hungry, stopping when full.
- Alert and observant of thoughts (hearing thoughts like "I'm so fat" and recognizing how these thoughts affect food choices).
- Diligent watchfulness of "pre" and "post" eating feelings (eating an ice cream cone prompts feeling good).
- Food is regarded as just being "what it is" rather than categorized as "good" and "bad" or "forbidden" foods.
- Nonjudgmental attitude toward the self. Self-worth is not based on weight, which helps a person make more mindful food choices.
- Mindful eating is an ongoing journey. Even when a person slips into mindless eating, he or she can get back on track rather than getting stuck in feeling "I blew it."

Types of Mindless Eating

Being as Unaware of Why You Eat as What You Eat

> *I am a mindless eater. I often get to the bottom of a bag of pretzels and think, "Wow, did I eat the whole bag? I don't remember eating that much." Or, I mindlessly grab a few handfuls of peanuts without really paying attention to how many scoops I eat. My roommate recently asked me if eating tortilla chips as a main course for breakfast was really a good idea. I didn't even realize this was my daily habit on days I have an early class.*

Mindless eaters eat out of unconscious habit or on autopilot. They are not consciously aware of, or ignore, the social, physical, or emotional cues that guide the decision to stop and start eating. Food choices and portions are often unbalanced, rigid, or not moderated. Decisions about what to eat are made without conscious thought, driven by emotions, or prompted by critical thoughts.

Mindless eaters are very responsive to external environmental cues rather than using their hunger as their guide. For example, they may not stop eating until people get up from the table. Or, they cease eating when the plate is clean rather than putting down their fork when their stomach is just satisfied. Feelings and thoughts can have an enormous amount of control in the lives of mindless eaters. Stress, boredom, and other negative emotions often steer the decision to stop and start eating.

For some people, zoning out from their body is the root of mindless eating rather than an emotional cause like problems with self-esteem. Mindless eating is like entering a trance. The body is moving without the guiding force of conscious thought. When the mind isn't fully present, a person can easily miss or ignore the body's cues of "Hey I'm full," or "I'm hungry," or the wisdom of the head saying, "We just ate a reasonable portion." They have trouble accurately assessing their hunger. They often don't know how to just cross over the line of "full" without going way past it.

It's not uncommon for mindful eaters to eat mindlessly every now and again. They may overindulge on sweets during a special occasion, when they go to a favorite restaurant, or on festive occasions such as Thanksgiving. As soon as they overeat, they know it because their body doesn't feel good, it's too full. They know they missed the mark and overfed their hunger. It happens and then the mindful eater just gets back on track. But mindless eating is problematic when it happens on a frequent basis, when it causes extreme weight gain, or if it is done in an effort to mend emotional hurt.

Mindless Eating Example

Let's say that a student is sitting at her desk studying. Unconsciously, she reaches for a box of crackers to snack on. This is her first mindless act. Because studying and snacking is part of her daily routine, she is not thinking about her hunger level. She pops one cracker after another mindlessly in her mouth. She doesn't even taste the individual crackers. She doesn't know even how the crackers make her feel as she eats them. As she eats the crackers faster and faster, she isn't aware that she has accelerated the pace. Perhaps she is reading a passage from *Hamlet* that she doesn't understand and feels overwhelmed. At this point, her body is full. When she reaches for the last cracker, she is suddenly aware that she has the very last cracker from the new box of crackers in her fingers ("Wow, when did I eat them all?"). Most mindless eating is unconscious because body and brain are not working together.

Eating on Autopilot

- Eating an entire plate of food and not tasting one bite. Munching on snacks while zoned out in front of the TV.
- Following "food rules" automatically, without thinking it through.
- Ignoring hunger or skipping meals even though hungry.
- Stress eating in situations such as exams, going home for the holidays, or roommate problems.
- Ignoring/inattentive to nutrition or getting a balanced variety of food.

- Multitasking while eating, such as snacking while studying, watching TV, driving, or talking and eating. Dividing one's attention between a task and eating.
- Unaware of portion sizes.
- "Grazing" on food. (mindlessly picking at a bread basket in a restaurant).
- Developing a food habit like routinely skipping breakfast.
- Ignoring bodily signs of hunger (stomach rumbling, low energy).
- Continuing to eat although full (stuffing rather than satiating hunger).
- Letting feelings control appetite.
- Member of the "Clean Plate Club." Eating everything whether you are hungry or not.
- "Live to Eat" rather than "Eat to Live" attitude (food is just about enjoyment and pleasure not a way to fuel the body).

Three Subtypes of Mindless Eating

There are three subtypes of mindless eating that college students generally face, which include mindless overeating, mindless undereating, and mindless chaotic eating. Each of these types brings unique challenges. It is important for every eater to identify his or her particular type of mindless eating. This will be helpful in knowing what aspects of behavior need the individual's full attention and awareness. It's also possible to have a combination of all three types of mindless eating.

Mindless Overeating—Nick

> *Everyone in my family is pretty heavy. They inhale their food. We could have gotten a group rate at all the gyms and weight watching programs we tried as a family. I remember going to the meeting and then we'd all come home and mindlessly devour a box of double stuffed sandwich cookies. My parents thought food was pretty much the cure for any ache or pain. Food was my Kleenex and my Band-Aids.*
>
> *In college, I was like a food junkie. I hid food. At night, I'd sneak out looking for snacks. During the day, I'd wait im-*

patiently for my roommate to go to class so I could eat in the privacy of my own room. Everywhere I turned there was food. One day, I got in trouble for smuggling food out of the cafeteria. My weight began to climb.

I mindlessly ate all the time. If I got a good grade on a test, I ate to celebrate. If I got a bad grade, it also gave me an excuse to eat to console myself. It really didn't bother me until I was at a party one night. Someone made a fat joke and everyone seemed to be looking at me. I don't know if they did or not but it felt that way. That's when I realized that my eating was a little out of control. I was so down. Any little problem made me feel like I was life's little hacky sack, just getting kicked around from one thing to another.

The following issues are involved in mindless overeating;

Awareness: Low awareness of or ignoring internal sensations. For example, doesn't stop when full or is conscious of feeling full but continues to eat anyway.

Observing: Notices feeling out of control, believes that she or he is unable to stop. Becomes distressed when mindless overeating occurs.

Shifting Out of Autopilot: Has difficulty shifting out of automatic habits and changing eating behavior. She or he routinely turns to food as a coping mechanism (stress eating). Eating habits are set on autopilot.

Being in the Moment: Eating quickly or rapidly lowers awareness of taste. Has difficulty checking in with his or her body when eating.

In the Middle: Trouble moderating eating or eating just enough to be satisfied. Measures of health aren't in the middle or normal range but at one extreme or the other such as high blood pressure, low energy, high cholesterol, etc.

Judgmental: Critical of self for overeating, feeling out of control, or mindlessly overeating. Feels embarrassed to eat in public, and therefore eats large amounts alone.

Acceptance: Feels uncomfortable with body image. Believes that success and failure is linked to weight. Lots of ups and downs in eating behavior.

Bingeing

Bingeing can be a part of mindless eating. It's an extreme version of unaware eating. Bingeing involves eating large quantities of food in a very short period of time. It's an amount of food that is larger than most people would eat in a similar amount of time or under similar circumstances. The food is sometimes eaten rapidly, to the point of feeling uncomfortable, and is accompanied by some distress—embarrassment, guilt, or self-disgust.

When people are compulsively eating, they tend not to be present physically or emotionally. They are in an "unaware" state. They may be trapped by guilty thoughts or they are in an emotional void. Eating numbs them out and provides a momentary escape from a painful feeling, experience, or thought. A binge detaches them from their body and they are barely aware of what they are putting into their mouth. They don't really taste or enjoy the food as they swallow it. A binge is a way of completely zoning out from feelings. So, one of the antidotes to bingeing and mindless eating is to stay "aware" and present while eating.

Sometimes people have what they "perceive" to be a binge versus an actual binge. The person may feel as if he or she overate but in actuality they did not eat more than a typical person would have consumed. Years of dieting and food rules have warped their perception of what a binge is. Almost anything feels out of control. For example, for someone on a low carb diet, eating a few pieces of bread may feel like a mindless binge. Yet, it isn't out of range with what a mindful eater would eat.

Mindless Undereating—Anna

In my hometown, I was a varsity athlete. I was always the coach's favorite and never thought about riding the bench. When it became apparent that I wasn't going to start, I began putting in more time at the gym and in practice work outs. Despite anything I did, nothing changed my standing on the team. I skipped meals to go to practice and work out. Things felt so out of control. I dropped a lot of weight really fast. This pattern continued for a few weeks. I didn't like the food in the dining hall so I only ate a few items over and over again. Yuck! It was like I had this bullhorn in my head constantly telling me what foods to steer clear of and to work harder. My world was reduced down to calories and fat grams. Every little bite led to worry and guilt. Foods I used to like were being erased from my world at an alarming rate. They had suddenly turned from luscious to fattening and dangerous in my eyes. Sure, I was always aware of my weight but what I experienced in my first year of college was a whole different ball game.

The following elements are involved in mindless undereating:

Awareness: Low awareness or ignores internal sensations. For example, ignores a rumbling stomach for the sake of the diet. Puts low emphasis on flavor, including tasteless diet food.

Observing: Notices feeling fat. At times, feels disgusted with his or her body.

Shifting autopilot: Has a routine of dieting, engages in repetitive rituals or strict habits with food. For example, eats only a certain brand of food or before a specific hour of the day.

Being in the moment: Doesn't experience the joy of eating in the moment. The positive experience is overshadowed by feelings of guilt. Worry about expectations and perfectionism distract from being able to enjoy the moment. He or she is often caught up in wondering if what they are eating is "right" or "wrong."

In the middle: Restricts food rather than eating a "normal" portion of food. Weight shifts. Instead of moderating intake of certain food groups, he or she drops or eliminates entire food groups (like dairy or meats). Overexercises. Inattentive to nutrition. Trouble moderating eating or eating just enough to be satisfied. Measures of health aren't in the middle or normal range, experiences health consequences for undereating.

Judgmental: Self-worth is affected by weight. Very critical of self even when losing weight.

Acceptance: Preoccupied and overly concerned with appearance and weight. Checks out people's bodies to compare. Has trouble accepting his or her own body and wishes for a friend's or movie star's body.

Hypervigilant Eating

Sometimes dieters and people struggling with mindless undereating say they are "overly aware" of what they eat. They stress out about every calorie and sweat about each bite. How can this be mindless eating? Hypervigilance is different from being aware because awareness is a nonjudgmental stance. It's kind of like the difference between watching someone and stalking them. The hypervigilant dieter is often very attentive to the calories and food but has turned his or her back to other important aspects of hunger, like taste, enjoying food, and feeling full.

Mindless Chaotic Eating—Jessie

High school memories, for some, bring back nostalgic thought of proms and football games. For me, it's visions of lunch tables and empty brown paper bags. Although I didn't have a name for it at the time, I learned about mindless chaotic eating in high school. At lunch, my friends and I sat around the lunch table sipping diet sodas and eating only Twizzlers. Then, we'd complain about being fat and give our lunches away to the guys. But it was my so-called best friend who took it to the next level. We'd go to my house and have a huge snack of Hostess cupcakes and ice cream because we were starving after ditching our lunch. We'd go to the bathroom and purge it out. My friend eventually stopped but I continued to sneak off after meals.

After I graduated, I went to an elite women's college. At first, my overeating and purging went away. But after a tough semester, I found myself mindlessly eating at dinner on the endless buffets. The cafeteria was a binger's worst nightmare and dream come true. Then, I'd wander from dorm to dorm in search of an empty bathroom stall.

One day, my resident assistant called a meeting to talk about the "problem person in the hallway." They didn't know who was purging in the bathroom and making a mess. The RA said the person was disgusting and disrespectful and didn't deserve to be in college if they couldn't clean up their own mess. I was so stressed out and embarrassed. I hoped no one saw the tears welling up in my eyes or my flushed cheeks. I wanted to stop. About a week later, I had a fight with my new boyfriend after freaking out that I might be pregnant. To my relief and horror, my doctor said I missed my period due to my erratic eating patterns.

Mindless chaotic eating involves the following elements:

Awareness: The *perception* of mindless overeating leads to a compensatory behavior (a type of purging) to get rid of an uncomfortable feeling. Conscious or unconscious awareness of difficult feelings (stress, hurt, etc.) leads to the desire to stop the feelings.

Observing: Does not want others to observe the behaviors. Hides mindless eating by consuming food in secret. May notice changes in body and symptoms associated with chaotic eating (gas, sore throat, stomach problems, and menstrual irregularities).

Shifting autopilot: An engrained habit of overeating and compensatory behavior that is difficult to change. Can engage of the behaviors and not really even be aware that he or she is doing it or doesn't give it much thought.

Being in the moment: Eating distracts from being in the moment. Turns attention away from uncomfortable feelings associated with eating, like being too full.

In the middle: Purchases large quantities of food. Difficult to maintain an even, balanced amount of food. A greater amount is eaten than another person would eat in the same situation or time frame.

Judgmental: Critical of self. Body shape and size dictates self-worth. Experiences rigid all or nothing thinking about food.

Acceptance: Difficulty accepting self and body as it is. Holds a continual desire for a different body.

Mixed Awareness

Chaotic mindless eating often affects awareness in two ways. The first kind is the type we already discussed with mindless overeating. As one is overeating, the person is not paying attention, ignores or misinterprets their body's innate natural cues about how to eat.

Purging also lowers awareness. The purging that accompanies chaotic eating often functions as a way of reducing the awareness of anxiety. For example, when a person perceives that they have overeaten, they may feel anxious. They may not know how to reduce their worry in healthy ways. They get stuck ruminating about how many calories they just consumed. The purging distracts from the anxiety. Purging is a very unhealthy way of dealing with the emotions.

Here are some of the excuses used for mindless/unaware eating: common rationales for clinging to mindless habits:

- I can't afford to buy healthy food.
- I don't like the food they have in the cafeteria.
- Someone ate all my food in the fridge.
- I'm too busy to eat healthily or mindfully.
- I don't have time to devote to healthy eating.
- I don't have a car so I can't go to the grocery store.
- I ran out of food points.

- I'm too stressed to eat healthily.
- I'm too tired and busy to change what I'm doing.
- No one cares what I eat.
- I'm healthy, it can't hurt me.
- I'll stop eating bingeing on candy after my exam.
- I can get away with skipping a meal and no one will really notice.
- There isn't anyone to go to dinner with me.
- Everyone else is eating the junk food.
- I'm an adult, I can eat what I want.
- I got up late and missed breakfast.
- I have to eat things I wouldn't normally to be social.

Chapter 2, Mindful Eating 101: To eat mindfully, step one is to identify what kind of mindless eater you are. Eating issues are not one size fits all, they fall along a continuum from mindful eaters to mindless eaters (mindless undereaters, overeaters, and choatic eaters). The pressures linked with a college environment and lifestyle may be an important factor in your shifting to different ends of this continuum.

Chapter 3

College Equals Mindless Eating?

You know you are a college student when…
Ramen noodles are one of the four major food groups.
Grilled ham and cheese is considered a balanced meal.
Buying anything more expensive than mac and cheese is considered splurging.
It's perfectly acceptable to eat cereal for breakfast, lunch, dinner, or all three.
A diet coke and M&Ms is a typical breakfast.
Computer paper doubles as a napkin and a placemat.
Heating up a frozen pizza in the microwave is considered serious cooking.
You consider your desktop to be a fine dining option.

Jokes like these poke merciless fun at college students' mindless eating habits. Although this might give us a little chuckle and sometimes hold a scary gain of truth, jokes like this suggest that it's quite "normal" to have unhealthy eating habits while in college. Granted, no one ever said college was a health spa, but these jokes make it sound as though the chance of having a well-balanced meal is slim to none. Despite the many hurdles, rest reassured that it is possible to eat mindfully in college.

Must College Equal Mindless Eating?

Contrary to popular belief, not every college student is a mindless eater. There are four factors that generally increase the likelihood that a student may struggle with mindless eating in college: *the school environment, personal risk factors, individual adjustment to the college transition, and lifestyle (sleep, stress, etc.)* Cooley and Toray 1996; DeBate, Topping, and Sargent 2001; Grassi 2001; Hesse-Biber and Marino 1992; Parham, Lennon, and Kolosi 2001; Racette, Deusinger, Strube, Highstein and Deusinger 2005). In order to address mindless eating habits, it's important to be *attentive* and *aware* of how each of these four aspects factor into one's life.

Let's say, for example, a student is typically a pretty mindful eater. However, to get to the cafeteria, he or she has to walk five miles in subarctic like weather. The only other alternative is a vending machine in the basement of the dorm. Unfortunately, snack foods in particular aren't very filling, which often leads many people to mindlessly eat. The challenge would be to find ways to cope with the very limited food options.

Or, perhaps the café nearest to the dorm is stocked full of healthy, organic cuisine. But, you have joined a sorority and you are required to eat at the sorority house for dinner despite their very unhealthy meal selections. Your concern would be a social issue rather than a problem with the nearest cafeteria. Or, maybe you only have afternoon classes and you tend to sleep through breakfast. By lunch, you are ravenous and find yourself overeating because you are starving. This mindless eating would be related to your lifestyle.

The Mindless Eating Environment

We will now discuss a number of food options, types of cafeterias (unlimited buffets vs. food courts), structure of food points, social events with food, amount of food available, emphasis on appearance at the college, plus college transition stress, including exams, roommate issues, competition, athletic pressure, stress, and academic pressure, among others. We will then go on to discuss personal risk factors such as perfectionism, mood disorders, rigid thinking, genetic predisposition, being overweight, and critical of self. Finally, we will discuss college lifestyle, including such factors as lack of sleep, social eating, buffets, pizza, freedom/independence, exposure to media/thin ideals, TV.

It is critical to take a good hard look at where you live and your dining enviornment. We are often quick to point the finger at ourselves for mindless eating without taking into consideration what is going on around us. Think of a fish swimming around in a polluted fish tank. The impact of the surrounding environment clearly must be considered in terms of the fish's health. Many people live in an environment that subtly promotes or discourages mindless eating, and they don't even realize it.

Each type of college education brings unique challenges to mindful eating, whether it's a liberal arts college, a public university, a private college, single sex, urban, or isolated, rural campus. For example, at some of the larger universities, there are only one or two cafeterias available for a residential tower of five hundred residents. It's tough to get a mindful, peaceful meal in this setting. An institution in a cold climate where it is difficult to get outside and exercise can lead students to snacking in front of the TV quite a bit more than they would if they could get out of the dorm and away from the fridge. In contrast, students I counseled in California expressed fear about getting into a swimsuit and going to the beach. The heat not only brought out skimpier clothing but it coaxed forth even more urgency to diet. If a student lives at home or in an apartment versus a residential dorm, then the demands of a cafeteria or mass-produced food don't affect him or her. Obviously, where you go to school and where you live is likely to affect how you eat.

Even small details of a cafeteria environment can make a significant difference to mindful eating. For example, one of my clients explained the layout of her college cafeteria. The food services workers scooped the entrees and side dishes onto her plate. She found that she couldn't just try a bite of this or a tiny sample of the new casserole on special. This serving style gave her no control over the portion size. Students said that they were likely to finish their entire plate anyway even if they were given more than they wanted, which often led to overeating. In addition, who hasn't gravitated toward the shortest food line rather than attempt to get what you really wanted? This can lead to a feeling of dissatisfaction and grabbing an additional snack later. At yet another university, cafeteria workers posted a sign stating "take what you want but eat what you take." Clearly, there was pressure not to waste food and to finish every bite on the plate. This is another subtle push toward mindless eating.

> Each year, the *Princeton Review* surveys students to rank the "best" and "worst" college campus food in the nation. See http://www.princetonreview.com

Mindless Eating and the College Transition

> *I first became conscious of my weight and dieting in my advanced math class. Prior to that, I never thought twice about calories. One day, my classmates and I were diligently working on algebra problems about weight. It was something to the effect of "if Jim weighs twice what Mary does and Jill is half the weight of Jim and Mary." The next question was about how many calories Tim would burn if he ate X amount of calories and ran for X amount of hours. I guess something just clicked in me. It primed my mind to think about things like calories and weight as something to manipulate. So, I made my own equation. If I went on a diet and ate X amount of calories and exercised X amount of hours how much would I weigh? I've been trying to stop working on that word problem ever since. It's so much more complicated than an A–B=*C.

So, what is it about college that makes it a prime time for mindless eating issues to appear? Is it the college food? Is it the competitive environment? Or, maybe it's the stress? Well, it's a little of all these things and more.

The pressure of college is one significant factor. Intense academic competition, whopping financial loans, relationships issues, being away from home, loneliness, parents' expectations, substance use, difficult roommates, and sexuality issues are just a few of the factors involved. Many of my clients have shared with me the enormous demands of college life. Tina, a junior in college, reported being verbally abused by her boss at her campus job. Her boss was also going to be her professor next quarter for a required class. Without the job, she couldn't afford to stay enrolled in college. Each day she juggled a job she hated, serious financial debt, and mountains of homework. She felt like one wrong step could ruin it all. Some students already have food issues before they arrive at college and the stressful environment just exacerbates or maintains a preexisting issue (Vohs, Heatherton, and Herrin 2001).

On top of all the stress that comes from being a student, once you enter college, you shoulder the sole responsibility for feeding yourself. It may sound like no big deal, but really it is. There are no longer parents to instruct and guide your food choices like reminding you to eat a piece of fruit or handing out granola bars. There's no longer a personal chef (aka your primary caregiver) preparing meals. Instead, you are in charge of every food decision and purchase.

Sometimes adding just one more responsibility can be too much. The added responsibilities can tip someone with the predisposition for eating issues over the edge. For example, let's say a person feels very out of control. She is frequently kicked out of her dorm room when her roommate has her boyfriend over, and she is struggling to pass one of her prerequisite classes. The pressure is too much but she doesn't know how to cope. Over- or undereating issues may emerge as a way to get back a sense of feeling in control. When a person feels in control of eating and body weight, it can be a substitute for feeling powerless within a chaotic and demanding environment.

College transitional factors include:

- First time away from home/added responsibility.
- Dating. The notion that appearance increases the likelihood of attracting dating partners.
- Pressure to succeed.
- Feeling lost (not knowing what to major in).
- Competition (academic, sports, leadership, internships, jobs).
- Access to unlimited amounts of food in dining halls.
- Fear/anxiety of the freshman 15.
- Stress (academic, financial, personal stress, transitional, relationships).
- Homesickness or transition problems (living with a roommate).
- Sports that emphasize weight and appearance such as gymnastics, diving, cross-country, etc.
- Certain majors and career choices which emphasize health and fitness may reinforce distorted views about eating and weight.
- Substance use.

What Causes Chronic Mindless Eating?

If you add a pinch of perfectionism, half a cup of body image dissatisfaction, a few spoonfuls of dieting, limited food choices, and stir in a lot of bombardment of media images idealizing thinness, what do you get? It's hard to say. No one knows the *exact* recipe or what makes one person more vulnerable than another to mindless eating and other eating problems in college. There isn't one factor we can point to. On the contrary, it's a complex combination of many physical, psychological, biological, and social factors (Jacobi 2005). Explaining how each dimension contributes to the problem could fill an entire bookshelf.

There are some general factors that increase the risk of developing eating issues. However, keep in mind that it is a combination of personality, genetic, social, and environmental variables and not one factor that causes mindless eating.

Personal risk factors for mindless eating include the following:

- Poor body image or unhappiness with one's body (not surprisingly, this turns out to be one of the most important factors for developing problematic eating).
- Genetics (history of being overweight, slow metabolism, overweight family members).
- Low self-esteem or feeling bad about oneself.
- Repeated dieting.
- Sensitivity to other people's opinions, difficulty making decisions.
- Highly self-conscious, particularly about appearance.
- Perfectionism.
- Control issues.
- Having a dysfunctional family.
- Feeling ineffective, inadequate, insecure, feel as if you have little control over your life.
- Early onset of puberty (part of puberty is gaining weight or early development of sexual characteristics before friends).
- Trauma (divorce, sexual abuse, grief, loss, emotional or physical abuse).

College Lifestyle Hazards That Inhibit Mindful Eating

Sure, college is a blast, but there are many aspects of day-to-day college life that make a person much more vulnerable to mindless eating. Little sleep and too much stress are two prime examples. In a sleepless, zombielike state, you're much less likely to care about the calories in a bag of chips when famished and exhausted. Or, when crunched to meet a deadline, mindful eating can really slip down on the priority scale. It even may feel like there's no time to swing by the drive-through to pick up a quick bite. Below are some candid quotes from students about how their college lifestyle frustrated their attempts to eat mindfully.

1. **Buffet style dining:** Buffet lines kind of remind me of cable TV. You can have a hundred TV stations to choose from and still feel like there is absolutely nothing on to watch. When I walk up to the buffet line, I'm overwhelmed by the sea of choices. Yet, some days I feel like there is nothing to eat. I find myself getting a little bit of this and a little bit of that and end up with a very strange combination of food. I tend to mindless eat more at buffets because I can't quite find what it is that will satisfy me and I worry that if I don't eat a lot that I am wasting money.

2. **Pizza:** My roommate and I signed up for what is called the "soup and bread program." It was our one volunteer activity. Once a week, our typical meal would be replaced with a wide selection of breads and various soups. The money they saved on a full meal was sent to a charity. However, 98 percent of the time we didn't do this. Instead, we ordered pizza and ate it mindlessly. But since it wasn't on our meal plan, I put it on my credit card. I'll be thirty and still paying off the pizza.
3. **Freedom to choose:** I became known as "sprinkle girl." Everything I ate had to have colored sugar sprinkles on it. It was like my seasoning salt. It didn't matter what food I put it on. Cake with sprinkles made sense. But I don't know why pasta with sprinkles, eggs with sprinkles, and tofu stir fry with sprinkles just appealed to me. The sprinkles made me eat more than I would have normally.
4. **Time issues:** I was totally off sync with the meal system. I'd study until two or three in the morning. Then, I'd get up around 10:30 a.m., way past breakfast hours. By lunch, I'd be starving and eat a huge meal. Since I ate such a large meal I typically wouldn't be hungry again until 8:30 p.m. so I'd miss dinner. Then, I'd mindlessly snack at night.
5. **Comfort foods:** I live for grilled cheese day. But, I have trouble eating these sandwiches mindfully. Grilled cheese transports me back to my inner kindergartener. When I see it on the cafeteria menu, I instantly go into a state of tranquility. Seven days of

meditation could hardly do the trick so well. For just a moment, I'm five again with not a care in the world besides watching TV and running up and down the hallways.

6. **Finances:** One day I got a candy bar out of a vending machine before my psychology class. To my surprise, the vending machine spit out my money, the candy bar plus twenty-five cents. I couldn't believe it. It was better than my birthday. I wondered if it was just a malfunction so I put my money in again. Like magic, it happened again. I was actually making money on my purchase. Was I that hungry for candy bars? No, but I was so strapped for cash. So, I cleaned out the machine and ate them all mindlessly. About a month later, I read about a study that was conducted at my university. It was a graduate student's dissertation on reinforcement schedules in psychology. In other words, when a behavior is reinforced, you are likely to do it again. When it is punished, generally, the behavior tends to decrease. This study tested the rate at which a person would continue to seek food when they obtained a reward. Note to self. Avoid the candy machines in the psych building.
7. **Stress:** My friends and I went out to dinner at an Italian restaurant to celebrate a birthday. When I got home, there was an annoyed and frantic message on my voice mail from my classmates asking, "Where are you, we are giving our group presentation right now." I thought it was the following day and it somehow slipped my mind! Luckily, I still had time to get to the oral presentation. The worst part was, during dinner, I had leaned forward against the table and as result I got butter on my shirt. I didn't realize I had greasy butter stains on my T-shirt where my chest hit the table. My professor insisted I take my coat off because it was so hot in the room. I was mortified as I gave an entire lecture with thirty pairs of eyes staring at the two greasy butter stains across my chest. When I came home, I was so embarrassed and stressed out that I started mindlessly shoveling food in my mouth. I wasn't the least bit hungry. I just didn't know how to get over the horror of the incident.

8. **Social eating:** The dining hall between 5:00 and 6:00 p.m. is basically a "meet and greet" session. There is practically assigned seating. We always sit in the exact same section of the cafeteria every night. I never used to drink coffee and eat donuts before I started college. I ate the glazed donuts mindlessly because I needed something to bide my time until my friends and I were done talking and drooling over the guys at the next table.
9. **Dehydration:** I lived in a house with a group of environmentally aware students. To save water, the house rule was to only flush if you really "needed" too. One day, one of my roommates dragged me into the bathroom, pointed to the toilet and asked, "is that your pee?" It was the color of a bright yellow-orange sunset. She handed me a bottle of water and made me solemnly vow to drink more water. Clearly, I wasn't drinking enough water nor was I eating enough water-filled fruits and vegetables. I tend to mindlessly eat granola bars and skip the fluids.
10. **Fast food/junk:** It's fast, but is it food? In a one mile radius, I have access to every kind of fast food option imaginable. I can buy a large meal for less than two bucks. It's more than I can eat but I can't seem to quit mindlessly eating fries which are my favorite.
11. **Sedentary life, no exercise:** If it was Tuesday or Thursday, I could sometimes get away with not even leaving the building. The pizza guy would deliver food right to me or I could coax my roommate into bringing something back for me. In high school, I played lacrosse and soccer. Now, trashcan basketball is my sport of choice. My mindless eating seems to have increased since I stopped being so active.
12. **Multitasking and eating:** My mindless eating comes from multitasking while I eat all the time. I study and eat. I drive and eat. John Montague, the Earl of Sandwich, was probably the first multitasking eater. Supposedly, the earl really loved to gamble, but refused to interrupt his fun for something as mundane as eating. To solve this problem, he ordered his servants to bring him meat and two pieces of bread. Thus, the sandwich was invented and the earl could continue his game and eat at the same time.

13. **Poor sleeping habits:** I need a lot more As and Zzzzs in my life. On average, I only get about five hours of sleep. I find that sometimes I mindlessly eat as a way to try to wake up.
14. **Alcohol and other substances:** My roommate gained a lot of weight our freshman year. She had a bad habit of ordering takeout at 2:00 a.m. after a night of partying. Drinking and smoking weed are a dangerous combo for getting the mindless munchies, among other negative consequences.

Here are some tips to help maintain mindfulness:

1. **Get some sleep:** A recent study found that people who get less sleep (below 7–8 hours) tend of have a higher body mass index (BMI) (Prinz 2004). There seems to be a connection between the hormones involved in regulating appetite and those related to sleep. Increasing the amount of sleep is such a tough thing to achieve for so many college students. Shaving off a couple of hours of snooze time each night is a pretty common practice. But, getting enough sleep is one of the most painless ways to help manage your weight. Be mindful of the importance of sleep—even an extra fifteen-minute nap. Observe how your body feels after pulling an "all nighter" versus a good night's sleep.
2. **Stay hydrated:** Eating mindfully is not just about eating, it is also about drinking. It's important to stay hydrated. People often confuse feelings of thirst with hunger, in other words they misread the body's cues. Also, being dehydrated can decrease energy and make you feel tired. It's easy to gravitate to food to try to get a quick burst of energy when what you really need is H_2O.
3. **Take a walk:** It's tough to fit in a little time at the gym when your work presses. Sixty-six percent of college students reported that they had a sedentary lifestyle, little to no exercise (Anding, Suminski, and Boss 2001). In another study, students reported getting less than three days a week of physical activity (Huang, Harris, Lee, Nazir, Born, and Kaur 2003). So, if you are having trouble exercising, you aren't alone. However, many students are starting to make exercise a top priority.

Try taking a "mindful walk." Break out of the power walking mode, and slow down. All of the senses should be used. Pay attention to the colors, smells, and sights along the way. Most students are so busy sprinting to class they may miss a lot of the scenery. When taking a mindful walk, it is important also to stay in the present moment and focus on the experience of walking. It is a quick and painless form of exercise and it gets the potential mindless eater out of his or her room, which is often the main location where mindless eating takes place.

> ***Chapter 3, Mindful Eating 101:*** Eating mindfully is not just about food, it's about the whole college lifestyle. All students should consider whether their lifestyle and personality make them more vulnerable to mindless eating. Taking care of your basic needs and paying attention to the influence of your environment will help you to eat more mindfully.

Chapter 4

The Urban Legend of the Freshman Fifteen

Fact or Fiction?

Spring Break in Mexico

What you are about to read is a "true" story. Really, it is. I heard this story from my roommate who heard it from her cousin. It happened to a student at a university in Texas. A group of seniors headed to Mexico for an entire week. It was their last Spring Break hoorah. They had the typical Spring Break agenda. Catch some rays and party until the wee hours of the morning. They knew some of the popular party hangouts could get a little seedy so they hung out mostly at the hotel. One night, Jim's girlfriend noticed he was missing in action. At first, she thought he might have gone to bed early. She found Jim an hour later sitting in a pool of his own blood.

Jim drank a little too much that evening. When he woke up, he was in a fog. Jim couldn't remember exactly what happened. He realized immediately that he was very cold. To his shock and horror, he was half naked in a bathtub filled with ice. Written on his chest in his own blood was "call 911." The doctors at the ER told him that his kidney had been removed. Luckily, he wasn't dead, but he learned that his kidney has been sold on the black market for a transplant.

Perhaps this story sounds vaguely familiar? Maybe you heard that this very same thing happened to someone from your campus? The details may have been just a little different. How about the student who was given a four point because her roommate died an untimely death during the year? If these tales do ring a bell, it isn't a surprise. These stories pass from university to university each generation. It doesn't really matter if you go to college in the north, east, south or west, these tales almost always come up in some form or another.

Stories like the one above are what are known as *urban legends*. These creepy, bizarre or scary stories exist in almost all cultures. They are told around campfires, whispered over coffee or late at night in dorm rooms. E-mail, faxes and Web sites have made the legends proliferate at light speed and across oceans. Most of these stories are credited to a secondary source that is suspiciously unable to be recalled or tracked down. If the tales begin with "a friend of a friend told me…" it should be your first clue to be wary. Despite the seven degrees of separation to the original source, the story teller typically vows it's 100 percent true. It's a little bit like the game of telephone. As the story passes from person to person, the details transform.

The Urban Legend of the Freshman Fifteen

No term has warped the beliefs and fears of college students more than *the freshman fifteen,* which has reached legendary fame. It has become an urban legend in itself. This chapter is devoted to the freshman fifteen because the idea of gaining so much weight plants a seed of fear in the minds of so many college students. This anxiety seems to damage rather than improve students' efforts to mindfully eat. Mindless eating is often blamed as the cause of this weight gain, yet, in some ways it seems to be the other way around. Anxiety about what is perceived as automatic weight gain in the freshman year can instigate mindless eating. This chapter will explain this phenomenon in more detail.

The Freshman Fifteen Story

Many male and female students share their story about gaining the freshman fifteen in fashion magazines, campus newspapers, or by word of mouth. Here is an example of a story told by one of my clients.

> *It was my first time moving away from home. The University of Colorado in Boulder was so much different from New York City. No smog, sky scrapers, taxis, or subway. It actually had green grass on the campus. I loved it! On weekends, I skied with my new friends in the mountains, hiked and hung out on the Hill, a great place to party. Although I was having the time of my life, I have to admit that I was a little overwhelmed by the change. I stopped playing a sport, I was eating a lot more junk food, and I had trouble sleeping due to an insomniac roommate. I never had to study in high school and I actually had to pull some serious all nighters to just pass. Of course, most of all, I missed my long-term boyfriend who went to college near home. So, I was doing a lot of comfort eating. Vending machines were like my twenty-four-hour food service. I confess that I did notice my jeans fitting a little more snugly. But, I shrugged it off. In the spring, when things calmed down, I vowed to exercise and drop the junk food habit.*
>
> *During the holidays, I flew home to New York. I craved the luxuries of home, namely my own private shower. As soon as I walked in the door, my mother says "Wow, you sure are eating okay. You put on weight." I know she was just making an observation but it freaked me out. Had I really put on that much weight? I sprinted to the nearest mirror to check myself out. One moment ago, I'd been happy as could be and the next minute I felt like a fat cow. I panicked. Stories about people gaining the freshman fifteen started flooding my brain. Didn't people warn me about eating too much? I read countless articles about this very thing! Oh my gosh, what if Tyler, my boyfriend, sees me like this? That*

moment started my drastic dieting. Although I had not gained even close to fifteen pounds, for some reason, it unleashed a host of my insecurities. I was sure it was fifteen pounds and there wasn't anyone or any scale that could change my mind.

Why It Could Be an Urban Legend

The freshman fifteen is suspiciously like an urban legend because it is a cautionary tale that warns students *not* to do something. It provides a strong, not so subtle warning to all college students to watch what they eat or they will balloon out. Unfortunately, a story about rapid and excessive weight gain is enough to frighten anyone. We already know that some students are scared to gain weight. Heck, most people are afraid to put on a few pounds. The legend has resulted in a large group of terrified students. They are worrying daily that the numbers on the bathroom scale will sky rocket. It's no surprise that a weight obsessed culture would create such a haunting tale.

Freshman Fifteen: Legend or Reality?

Is the freshman fifteen really true or is it just a tale? Many students don't really know and don't want to find out the hard way. The research below suggests that the freshman fifteen fits the definition of a legend in many ways. Some students gain weight but it is often blown way out of proportion.

Almost Everyone Knows What the Term Freshman Fifteen Means

Reality: The freshman fifteen is part of our cultural vernacular. Over 90 percent of freshman surveyed can easily define it (Graham and Jones 2002). The term *freshman fifteen* is so well known that it has become a mainstream term that pops up over and over again in the media.

It's even the title of a book, *Fighting the Freshman Fifteen* by Robyn Flipse et al. (2002), which is a nutritional guide for college students. No wonder college students are so freaked out about it. Every time they turn around there is another warning about how much weight they will gain the moment they enter college.

College Students Experience Some Weight Gain

Reality: In general, yes, many students gain weight. The majority of studies point to approximately a five-pound increase for women and around a seven-pound increase for men (Anderson, Shapiro, and Lundgren 2003; Cooley and Toray 1996, 2001; Graham and Jones 2002; Hodge, Jackson, and Sullivan 1993; Levitsky, Halbmaier, and Mrdjenovic 2004; Levitsky and Youn 2003). So, many freshmen do gain weight but on average it is often below the legendary fifteen pounds.

Everyone Gains Weight in College

Legend: According to a study by Dr. Melody Graham and Amy Jones, of the 110 freshman subjects in their study, 36 percent actually lost weight. Hodge, Jackson, and Sullivan (1993) found no change in the mean weight among the freshman women they surveyed during a six-month period. Thus, not everyone gains weight in college.

Weight Gain Is Just for Freshmen

Legend: It's not just about being a freshman. Weight gain and loss can happen at any time during one's college career or life for that matter (Anderson et al. 2003; Cooley and Toray 2001). Shifts in weight often happen during periods of transition (puberty, going to college, having a baby, middle age, etc.). In addition, weight gain may not happen all at once but can accumulate over the four years of college. This is particularly a problem for students who have weight issues before they even arrive at an academic institution (Racette, Deusinger, Strube, Highstein, and Deusinger 2005).

Dorm Food Is Completely Responsible for People Gaining Weight

Legend: David A. Levitsky, professor of nutritional sciences and psychology at Cornell, found that all you can eat buffet options accounted for approximately 20 percent of the weight gain freshmen experienced during the first twelve weeks at college (Levitsky, Halbmaier and Mrdjenovic 2004). The rest of the weight gain is due to other lifestyle factors like skipping healthy foods, lack of sleep, stress eating, missing breakfast, and bingeing on unhealthy foods. Levitsky found that students eat an estimated 174 more calories than they burned in a day.

Unfortunately, buffet style dining is still common in academia. This kind of dining option is a huge challenge for mindless eaters. A single swipe of a card gives access to an unlimited amount of food. Levitsky's study of college dining found that students eat on average 250 more calories when eating buffet style (Levitsky et al. 2004).

Men Are Not Concerned About Gaining Weight

Legend: College men also report worrying about their weight and shape, followed rules about eating, and limited their food intake (O'Dea and Abraham 2002; Olivardia, Pope, Mangweth, and Hudson 1995). Many males are very concerned and worried about gaining the infamous freshman fifteen

Worrying About Gaining the Freshman Fifteen Will Help Prevent It

Legend: Worrying about gaining weight is actually a pretty ineffective way to prevent weight gain. Graham and Jones (2002) found that "freshmen who were concerned about gaining 15 pounds were more likely to think about their weight, have a poorer body image than others and categorize themselves as being overweight" (172).

Lack of Nutritional Education Is Completely Responsible for Weight Gain

Legend: Some believe freshman weight gain may be in part due to students' lack of knowledge about the basic principles of nutrition, metabolism, genetics, and human physiology. Research shows that a formal education in nutrition does seem to help some students manage their weight (Cousineau, Goldstein, and Franko 2004; Matvienko, Lewis, and Schafer 2001).

American Food and Food Culture Contributes to the Problem

Reality: Although not entirely to blame, American culture seems to contribute to weight gain in many ways. Portion sizes, dieting obsessions, fast food, and junk food all play a significant role. David Holben, an assistant professor of human and consumer sciences at Ohio University, conducted a study with graduate student Hsin-Fen Chen (2000) to examine whether international students experienced weight changes in college. According to the results of their study, noted in the *Journal of the American Dietetic Association*, the international students gained an average of three pounds and their body fat rose about 5 percent after only twenty weeks of school. The students in the study noted that they had more access to an unlimited amount of food, ate foods their bodies were not accustomed to, and had heavier meals than in their home countries.

Why Do Students Gain and Lose Weight?

So, as you can see from the research, yes, lots of college students do gain weight during their first year of college. This is true. Every fall high school graduates head for college to juggle a difficult academic load and create a new social life. As if that weren't demanding enough, they take over mom's or dad's job of meal planning and making sure basic needs are met, a task that they may not have had to worry about before. The stress of handling rigorous studies and being away from parents for the first time, in an environment with unlimited access to snack food, pizza, and alcohol and a low activity level, can quickly result in weight gain. In circumstances like these, gaining weight is a very real possibility.

Other students experience a weight drop. No more home cooked meals, pans of mom's chocolate peanut butter brownies, or a well-stocked open pantry. The limited access and structured schedule definitely helps some people maintain a more routine eating schedule. For once, an on the go, high-achieving student actually might slow down, have a seat with friends, and eat a healthy, well-balanced meal. An increase in activity level also makes a difference. A student might walk an extra few miles to class, hike up a couple of flights of stairs with a heavy backpack, or take part in a pick up game on the quad. These students ultimately lose weight.

Remember that weight gain and loss varies by *individual.* This really can't be stressed enough. Some people will gain weight, some people will lose weight, but it's important to remember that each person's experience is unique.

The Freshman Fifteen

What's the Big Deal?

Keeping the freshman fifteen urban legend alive is a bad idea for several reasons. First, warnings about gaining the freshman fifteen don't appear to inspire healthier behavior. It hasn't scared students into dropping junk food nor has it motivated them to eat their fruits and vegetables. So, it seems to be ineffective in changing behavior. Unfortunately, the term appears to be more successful in raising weight anxiety, which we know leads to more eating problems.

The freshman fifteen legend also hurts students by creating a "self-fulfilling prophecy." When we believe something will happen, unconsciously, our behavior tends to lead us in that direction. For example, a student might say to herself, "I feel like I am bad at math and will probably fail my math exam." She is then likely to subconsciously act in ways that match that belief. She doesn't study, she goes out the night before the exam, and skips some classes. Surprise, surprise, she fails the exam. In the same vein, a student who's convinced he will gain the freshman fifteen, is more likely to eat in a way that will make it happen. For example, he might find himself filling up his plate, getting a second helping, and eating extra desserts. Basically, if you think something is going to happen, you shouldn't be surprised if you start acting in ways that will make it more likely to come to fruition.

The final downside to the freshman fifteen story is that it makes gaining weight a "normal" behavior. If the "norm" is putting on fifteen pounds then people may believe they are suppose to gain weight because hey it's part of the college experience. A person might subconsciously start behaving in ways to meet the norm to be "normal." Given what we know about the power of expectations, the freshman fifteen legend may do more to promote mindless eating and weight gain than it does prevent it.

Thinking Mindfully About the Freshman Fifteen

Aware: When friends and family chitchat about the freshman fifteen, pay attention to your gut feelings. Is your response anger, irritation, or does it perhaps raise your anxiety level a notch or two?

Observe: It's important to just listen and make a mental note each time you hear people tearing down their body or obsessing about weight. Consider how and in what context talk of the freshman fifteen comes up. Was it said as a warning or as a judgment?

Looking at the gray areas: Make sure to educate people. Remind your friends and family that most studies show that on average the weight gain is about five to seven pounds depending on your gender, height and body shape. Remember weight gain and loss varies by *individual.*

Shift out of autopilot: Without reading this book, most people wouldn't give the freshman fifteen a second thought. People are so nonchalant about the topic that they don't stop to think about what it means or how they talk about it. When speaking about weight issues, it's important to do so thoughtfully and mindfully. Steer clear of perpetuating the idea and expectation that everyone gains weight in college. Instead, when someone uses the term *freshman fifteen*, confront them about their choice of words. Role model a healthier slant on the subject by focusing on health, exercise, eating mindfully, and improving eating habits.

Nonjudgment: The freshman fifteen is a highly judgmental phrase when used to tease or describe someone's weight gain. It's very important to avoid using this term and instead be compassionate. Try empathizing with how tough it is for college students to experience shifts in their weight when they enter college. Acknowledge what a challenge it is to eat mindfully in a college environment that has unlimited buffets and academic pressure.

Acceptance: We have to accept that the notion of the freshman fifteen isn't going to drop off the face of the universe. Our culture creates itself through its language and the stories we tell. Try creating a positive urban legend that encourages college students to eat mindfully and feel good about their weight and body image. How would the story spread? What would be the underlying message of your story?

Chapter 4, Mindful Eating 101: The freshman fifteen is a legend we tell students to raise their anxiety about gaining weight during college. In actuality, some students gain weight and some lose weight. To inspire healthier behavior in yourself and others, it would help to stop using this term and start talking in positive, mindful ways about nutrition and health.

Chapter 5

Your "Relationship" With Mindless Eating

During the first semester of college, my friends invited me to participate in what I can only call a sugar orgy. We gorged ourselves mindlessly with cream filled vanilla cupcakes with stiff chocolate icing and sugar powdered donuts washed down with instant hot chocolate topped with fake marshmallows. After that day, my friends and I continued to mindlessly eat from time to time. We pigged out on pizza and made late night runs to any fast food place open past midnight. Mindlessly eating with my friends unknowingly convinced me that it was "okay." It seemed like no one else was worried about it.

Friends and family have a knack for bringing out the best and worst in us. If you're lucky, the people you care about encourage you to be the healthiest individual you can be. If you aren't so fortunate, your loved ones can do just the opposite. They undermine your efforts to live a healthy lifestyle, nurture your body, and eat mindfully. While reading this chapter, it's important to bring all of your relationships to the forefront of your awareness—friends, roommates, sisters, brothers, crushes, sorority sisters, and partners. The goal of this chapter is to become more aware of the parallel between your relationship with food and how you relate to people.

Whine and Dine

Eating plays a pivotal role in our social lives. Unless a student is a commuter or lives off campus, it's likely that he or she will eat with a group of friends every single day. It's common for students to sit for hours commiserating about the unpalatable food and coming up with increasingly more inventive food pairings from the serve yourself line. Mealtimes are a good opportunity to compare notes, moan about tough professors, and check out the very attractive person sitting at the next table. So, we have to keep in mind that there is a lot more going on at mealtimes than just eating food.

Eating is such a social event that many of us feel it is essential to eat with another person. Sometimes we are even afraid to eat alone. You might worry that people will look at you as if you are freakishly weird if you eat by yourself. Anyone who has ever considered bringing a book as a dinner companion rather than going it solo, knows what I'm talking about.

Are You Going to Eat That?

Dining with friends is one of the many perks of college life. However, friends might have a greater influence than you realize on how much and what you eat. In fact, attitudes about food and eating are often shared by groups of women who are close, and other groups of people who spend time together (Gilbert and Meyer 2004; Hoer et al. 2002). If you are a member of a healthy group of friends, that's good news because you are more likely to share their positive attitudes about eating. But, if you are surrounded by chronic dieters, watch out. This could be a bit more of a challenge. The group dynamics can set mindful or unhealthy expectations about what to eat and look like.

Don't get me wrong, your dinner companions can have negative *and* positive influences on your dining habits. For example, Hausenblas and Carron (1998) examined the eating patterns of college students living in dorms. Thankfully, the researchers discovered that friends, for the most part, do help each other to adopt healthier eating habits. None of the participants in the Hausenblas and Carron (1998) study reported that their hall mates introduced any problematic eating behavior like purging or severe restricting of calories. Although it did not happen in this study, many people do learn unhealthy, even dangerous, eating behaviors from those around them. My counseling clients have reported many stories of friends who taught them how to diet in dangerous ways. Sometimes they weren't really even aware that they were picking up the harmful behavior until it was too late. It's easy to unconsciously mimic the behavior of those around us.

You can't help but sneak a peak at what other people are eating. It's just like checking out what your friends are wearing or comparing how much time everyone spends doing homework. If the person on your right, is eating a large salad and to your left another friend is eating a fruit plate with turkey on a whole wheat roll, consciously or unconsciously you may feel pressure to eat in a similar matter. Equally, if everyone is reaching for a heaping pile of unhealthy snacks, it might not seem unusual to eat a few candy bars: these are both examples of food peer pressure.

Keeping Up With the Joans

> *My first day at college, I could hardly contain my excitement about meeting my new roommate. We had never met face to face but we had spoken on the phone periodically throughout the summer. We had been matched up by an extensive computer survey. Thankfully, we clicked immediately. We seemed to have a lot in common. As soon as I opened the door, my excitement fizzled. There she was, skinny as a rail with jeans hanging low on her waist and her midriff displaying amazing abs. Instantly, I disliked her. It's funny, she didn't sound skinny over the phone! Before I moved in with my new "perfect" roommate, I wasn't madly in love with my thighs but I could live with them. But, day by day I noted that my normal, secure self was slipping*

away. My roommate, obviously is a twig but she doesn't know it. I thought to myself, if she thinks she's fat, I wonder what she's thinking about me?

Almost all of us have felt like this woman at one point or another. We've felt inadequate and envious of someone else's body. We've compared our dress sizes, abdominal muscles, cheekbones, hair lengths, eye colors, and weight.

This tendency to compare and be competitive is actually quite a serious problem. It's so alarming that researchers have extensively studied the competitive nature of eating and body image among teenage girls and women. These studies have found that females who admit to chronically comparing themselves to others are more likely to be unhappy with their body images (Faith, Leone, and Allison 1997; Thompson, Coovert, and Stormer 1999).

The Starve Wars: Are You a Competitive Eater?

Here are some signs you are at risk of becoming a *competitive eater*:

- I don't change in front of my friends because I don't want them to see my body.
- I'm envious of my friends' bodies. I wish that I could look more like them.
- I compare the size of certain body parts with my friends' bodies to see how mine size up.
- I make critical comments about other people's bodies, but in reality, the snide comments come out of jealousy or fear.
- When I'm with someone who has a larger frame, I feel better about my own body. When I'm with someone smaller than I am, I feel uncomfortable.
- If my friend looks better than me, it upsets me.
- I don't eat junk food in front of other people, even if they are eating it.

- I make sure that I order less food or lower calorie meals than my friends when I'm at a restaurant.

Sororities and Social Groups

Ever heard the "marker story?" According to this story, women pledging "hell week" are forced to stand naked in a line. The members of the sorority walk down the line and circle with a big, black permanent marker any areas of fat on the women's bodies. It's a humiliating and graphic story of women's worst fear. Whether or not this hazing incident actually happens on many college campuses is irrelevant. The fear of being socially rejected based on body shape and size has many forms. What's interesting is that the discrimination is done by other women. Judgments are sometimes harsher among individuals of the same sex versus the opposite sex.

Research on Sororities

Women in sororities do seem to have an elevated risk for developing eating issues according to some studies (Allison and Park 2004; Hoerr et al. 2002; Schwitzer, Rodriguez, Thomas, and Salimi 2001). For example, Allison and Park (2004) examined the eating habits of freshman women as soon as they started school. At this point, they didn't find too much difference between the eating habits of women who were about to pledge a sorority and women who decided to live as independents. Unfortunately, check in with those same women when they are about to graduate and you'd find a different situation. Among women in sororities there was much greater incidence of and struggles with eating concerns than among women who did not join sororities.

This brings up the whole chicken and the egg dilemma. We really don't know if women prone to watching their weight are attracted to sororities or if sororities themselves are encouraging women to focus more on dieting and watching their weight. Perhaps sororities emphasize appearance or teach women how to conform to certain rules. For example, some organizations set rules about wearing Greek letters on certain days. Or, maybe there is social pressure to look a certain way because the woman's identity is associated with a particular group (e.g., a sorority may have the reputation of having attractive women). Pressure may also be related to the group meals that are set at some sorority houses at large state universities. Although there are many possibilities, what we do know is that women who are in sororities are often at more risk for developing disordered eating habits.

Antimindful Behavior

> *"How many cookies do you think I can fit into my mouth?" my frat brother inquired as he stuffed in the fifth Oreo. My competitive juices started flowing as he started to grab another cookie. Bet I can make it six, I challenged. Any double dog dare he threw my way, I took. One night I almost went to the emergency room after eating six fire hot buffalo wings. I wasn't going to back down on proving that I had an iron clad stomach.*

Collegiate men, as well as women, have their fair share of mindless behavior, much of which seems to focus on social eating and drinking. One of my male clients told me about "the burrito challenge." It involved a group of close friends competing to stuff down the most burritos during the course of lunch. His frat brothers, of course, did not know about his mindless eating problems. He didn't join in this "challenge", and for the next week, his frat brothers called him every name in the book—wimp, loser, and worse. His story highlights how sometimes mindless behavior is part of the social fabric of day-to-day collegiate life.

Eating contests, binge drinking, and food related hazing (eating gross things) are all examples of mindless behavior that can become competitive and used to attain social status. For the most part, mindlessly eating burritos isn't going to hurt you physically—if you don't count indigestion. However, certain substances, if consumed mindlessly or competitively are psychologically and physically dangerous, even lethal. It's important to notice whether mindless behaviors are being embraced like excessive eating, drinking, or sex, and, on the other hand, whether a mindless behavior is being thought of as a social or honorable behavior.

Family Members

> *When I was growing up, my mom was what I called a diet-aholic. She fell on and off the dieting bandwagon all the time. Sometimes, she'd suddenly decide that we were all on a diet and would serve weird concoctions of tasteless food. At other times, she would bake mountains of cookies, cakes, boxes of donuts, and cook enormous casseroles. Then, she'd tell me that I'd need to go on a diet because I was getting chunky. She projected a lot of her weight insecurities onto me. I know my mom isn't to blame for my mindless eating issues, but her tendency to place a lot of importance on weight didn't help matters too much.*

Family members play a significant genetic, social, and psychological role in the way we eat. You share the same DNA and your bodies bear some similarity in shape and size to those of family members because there is a significant genetic component to body shape, size, and weight—family members are probably around the same height, for example. They may also carry body fat in similar locations on their bodies; for example, the majority of extra weight might be carried on stomach or thighs. Exercise and eating habits influence how genetics are expressed and may make you thinner or heavier than other family members. DNA just plays a part in creating the range of what a person's body can possibly do.

In addition to the role of genetics, etiquette at the dinner table teaches you a lot about how you think and feel about food, showing you how to prepare meals and telling you what to eat or not eat. This may not have been in the form of explicit instructions, but information you absorbed from taking mental notes on what kind of groceries are in the fridge or absent from the cupboards. Maybe you grew up in a family of "health nuts" where everything you ate was organic. Or, perhaps you had a sister who was always on a fad diet who taught you to feel guilty after eating a sweet. Or, maybe you had a dad who brought home donuts every Sunday morning. All these elements can instruct and influence you in regard to routines and rituals around food. Basically, it's likely that your food tastes and habits reflect those of your primary caregivers.

Families impact people in another way. Mental health issues may make you more vulnerable to developing eating issues. Symptoms of depression, for example, include loss of appetite, but can also involve overfeeding. It's also important to consider family dynamics and how they may contribute to eating issues. No, family members are not to "blame" for eating problems but they do have an important psychological influence. For example, imagine a child from a very controlling family. The girl's family tells her who to date and what career to choose. The child may gravitate toward an eating issue because it is the only aspect of her life that her family cannot control.

Isolation and Eating Issues

For some people, college can be a pretty isolating, lonely event. Parents, childhood friends, and one's familiar, comfort zone are left behind. Suddenly, your social world must be reorganized. A sophomore at an Ivy League college got stuck in the "dismal dorm" on the outskirts of the campus. Her friends were on the main campus. They were not willing to trek out to her dorm in no-man's-land. She spent a very lonely year in a dorm without any close friends.

Isolation is a real problem for some college students and it can be a setup for people who have an eating concern. Food is sometimes used as a reliable source of comfort. It can keep a person feeling safe and good even when people are a disappointment. One of my clients described food as her "best friend" and "worst enemy." Food was always there to help her out. Eating made her feel better. When people have real trouble moderating their eating, they tend to have a lot of difficulty being social and maintaining relationships because eating is such a social event. A person struggling with extreme mindless eating, for example, often seeks solitude to hide her or his eating issues.

Even dieting can interfere with relationships and being social. A serious high protein dieter wouldn't be caught dead in a pizza joint. If the high protein dieter does go along with the group, it's likely that he or she will talk incessantly about the evils of simple carbohydrates. Who can enjoy pizza with annoying talk like that? Instead of enjoying the pizza, the group may feel uncomfortable about the choice of restaurant or the high protein dieter. Do you think that the pizza hater will be included again? Dieting and diet talk aren't the best ways to make friends on campus.

Mindfulness of Boundaries

When I let out too much about my past, I feel like I'm "leaking." As if all my personal issues are pouring out of me and I can't find a stopper to plug up the hole.

For people with mindless eating issues, setting appropriate boundaries with the people in their life can be a real challenge. Boundaries are the invisible emotional lines that we draw between ourselves and other people. People draw many different kinds of boundaries—emotional, physical, sexual, spiritual, in relationships, and at work. For example, you create a limit on how much time you spend with friends so you can get homework done. Boundaries provide protection, they prevent people from walking all over you, taking advantage, or hurting you emotionally. The lines also help you to know and clearly separate out where you end and another person begins. Sometimes we create boundaries in very concrete ways. For example, roommates may decide that there is no sharing of clothes or food. Other times, boundaries are set by shutting a door or by not answering a question.

College students renegotiate many boundaries with their parents when they start school. They set the number of times they will talk by phone and choose who will control the finances. Prior to college, parents create many of your boundaries for you. They teach you how much it is appropriate to share, when to call it a night through curfews, and when to stop and start eating.

How to Mindfully Create Boundaries

To establish boundaries, it's a matter of finding an emotional and psychological skin that will be protective yet allow you to breathe and be close to people. You let friends into your world, cautiously and mindfully. When that boundary is violated, it is clear immediately and it causes discomfort. It's a little bit like someone standing too close. They have invaded your boundary or personal space.

RELATIONSHIP BOUNDARIES

Very Rigid ------------------------	Appropriate --------------------	Loose Boundaries
Doesn't let anyone in	Lets in some people who seem trustworthy	Lets everyone in
Overly/ very protective of self	Protective	Low protection
Distrustful/very cautious	Thoughtfully trustful	Overly trustful
Very private	Shares private things with close friends	Shares everything

Figure 5.1 Relationship Boundaries

Relationship Boundaries: These are limits you set with others about how to treat you and how you will behave around others. People need boundaries to create limits that will ensure their safety. Some people put up tight boundaries that keep people away whereas others have very open boundaries with few limits. A healthy boundary keeps you protected and clearly defines an appropriate, comfortable level of closeness.

1. **Mindfully create work and relationship boundaries:** When you are buried under a stack of papers, tests, and final exams, making time to be with family, partner, or friends can be really difficult. Because time is limited, you need to concentrate on the time that can be spent with them. But when you are with loved ones, it's important to leave college stress behind, and just be with them—make eye contact, touch, own those moments. Then, it will not seem as though other people are "taking time" away from you. Reduce the quantity of time, maximize quality.
2. **Knowing when to say no:** It's okay to say *no!* Sometimes people are afraid to say no because they think that people will not like them. But we all have a right to say no and it's important to be true to your own needs. If saying no is a problem, then you may want to take some time to reflect on what you fear will happen as a result of a refusal. Ask yourself, what is the worst case scenario?
3. **Knowing when to say yes:** People who tightly maintain their boundaries often don't know when to let people in. They like to do things themselves and have a very hard time asking for help. They are afraid of asking for things because they fear that they will be a burden. It's okay to ask for help. We all need other people to give us a hand once in awhile.
4. **Creating physical space:** In order to maintain good relations with other people, it is important to acknowledge how much physical and emotional space you need. Some people enjoy hugs and being physically close, while other people need a lot of physical space. State your boundaries in clear terms rather than hinting (rather than avoiding a phone call from someone you don't want to see

or moving someone's hand away rather than telling them directly that you feel uncomfortable).

5. **Creating privacy:** There is a natural progression in the way we get to know people. We start out with fairly superficial information like name, age, and basic demographics and work our way to a little more personal information like religion, political views, morals, daily stressors, to finally very personal information such as problems with your families, disorders, traumas, secrets, why you broke up with an ex. It's very rare that you move through this progression in a single meeting. It's helpful for you to know your comfort level and whether you let people in too quickly or keep them at arm's length.

Food Boundaries

Whether you know it or not, we also create boundaries in our relationship with food. In fact, the boundaries you set with people often mirror the lines you draw with food. People who restrict their eating often create a boundary that is sometimes too impermeable and rigid—absolutely no cookies. The boundary also extends to their bodies. A fragile body says don't get near me and often such people have difficulty being touched or being intimate. They frequently avoid conflict because it would mean disclosing something that is bothering them or letting someone in a little.

Overeaters have the opposite problem. Their food boundary is too loose. They have difficulty setting appropriate limits. Too much food comes in. They work on impulse because there isn't the boundary that keeps them in check or their cravings contained. They often have loose relationship boundaries, or they don't filter out enough people. Sometimes it is being intimate with acquaintances instead of just those that they have a close bond with or a serious dating relationship. Or, maybe it is sharing too much personal, private information with someone they just met. With food, it feels as though too much is coming in, or the boundary is too open.

Creating Food Boundaries

We work very hard to find just the right boundary, whether it is with people or food. A healthy food boundary is one in which food is allowed to come in or be eaten but it includes limits. For example, it would mean allowing ourselves to have dessert, but putting a set portion size on it. A piece of cake rather than the whole cake.

How to Eat More Mindfully With Friends and Family

Aware: Choosing your dinner companions mindfully—Do you want to eat?

Questions to ask oneself:

1. When I eat with friends or family, does it ever make me feel uncomfortable/ashamed? Do they make me strive to eat more healthily?
2. Do I participate in healthy (daily events, harmless gossip, and academic concerns) vs. unhealthy (talking about feeling fat, criticizing the food) table talk?
3. Have I ever been involved in taking an informal vote to make a collective decision about what we all would or would not eat ("I'll have dessert only if everyone else does")?
4. Are my friends or family ever covertly or overtly competitive (bragging about their diet or weight)?
5. Would you rather eat alone or in secret because you don't want other people to see what you're eating?
6. Do you ever eat in secret or eat again after you leave a friend because you think he or she will judge you?
7. Do you look to other people as a standard concerning what and how much to eat?

Observe: Notice how often we give food as a sign of how we feel about someone. Sometimes, for mindless eaters, this encourages the connection between food and love. Instead of care package full of goodies, ask to be sent some nonfood items. Let parents, grandparents, and friends know it is a better idea is to send you a roll of quarters, a box of laundry detergent/Kleenex, gum, energy bars, special soap, a gift certificate to a store like the Body Shop, a magazine subscription, towels, gift certificates to a restaurant, socks, movie passes, coffee, a special picture from home, a greeting card sent from your pet at home via the help of your parent, a small erase board, a throwaway camera, a pack of Post-It notes, a work of fiction, The Questions Book which is great for late nights and boredom, stamps, a piggy bank with a handful of quarters, printer paper, a ticket for a concert, a gas card, and most important—a personal note of encouragement.

Looking at the gray areas: If your social calendar gets top heavy on dinner dates, it may be time to consider going to a movie (without the dinner), doing homework together, taking a walk, or getting coffee.

Shift out of autopilot: Mealtimes can become so rigid and predictable that it attracts attention if you eat a steak sandwich instead of your typical turkey sub. It's worth trying something completely unusual like bringing a cup of gourmet coffee to a study group instead of chips or suggesting a new location to meet.

Being in the moment: Mindless eating can be contagious. Try to be wary of falling into food peer pressure (eating just because other people are), and try to sidestep it by really assessing your hunger level. Ask yourself, am I eating because of real hunger or because my roommate is digging into the Tostitos right now?

Nonjudgment: Help other people by role modeling a positive, mindful attitude toward eating. Practicing compassion toward yourself is an important aspect of avoiding mindless eating.

When a critical thought shows up, label it as a judgmental statement. Insert statements like "it's okay to eat," "it's not easy to eat mindfully," or "I'm really trying hard, it's okay if I'm not perfect."

Acceptance: It is very challenging to accept that friends and family can inhibit mindful eating. It's easy to feel that loved ones "should" be better at supporting your efforts to eat more mindfully and be the perfect dining companions. Alas, our friends and family are only human. It is difficult for them to separate out their own eating issues so that they are also able to support other people's eating issues. Understanding and acceptance that friends, partners, and family members aren't perfect helps you to utilize their support more effectively. It's about learning to take the supportive statements and let go of the not so helpful mindless eating feedback. Rather than vowing never to eat with them again, it is more helpful to open up a dialogue about mindful eating.

> ***Chapter 5, Mindful Eating 101:*** Friends and family members can help or hinder your efforts to eat more mindfully. So, it's important to be mindful of who you invite to dinner. The positive role models should be kept close by and attempt to steer clear of people who sabotage mindful eating. If you can't avoid mindless eaters, just be conscious of their influence on your mindful eating.

Chapter 6

The Body Image Blues

Body Goggles

There's a poster that never fails to catch my eye. Although I am chronically late for my geology class, I take a quick glance at it as I'm sprinting by. The poster has three images of a guy at a party. The photos are taken at various times during the night, 8:30, 10:30, and midnight. He looks distinctly different in each picture.

In the 8:30 picture, the guy is pretty unattractive. In fact, the person who photographed this poster purposefully tried to make him ugly. You can tell he's not as unattractive as they make him out to be. His zits are magnified, his hair is ruffled, and he has a goofy look on his face.

In the next picture, he's the spitting image of a pretty normal, average guy. It looks very natural. He's smiling. I always think to myself that he is the kind of guy I'd notice at a party and stealthily work my way over to him. However, I would do some research on his vital stats—age, major, if he had a girlfriend—before maneuvering closer later in the night.

In the final picture, Mr. Poster Guy is drop dead gorgeous. He's unrealistically good looking and suspiciously perfect. The photographer must have airbrushed it and cleaned up every blemish. There was not a pore in sight or a crooked hair on his shiny head. He is smiling like he's in a toothpaste commercial and there is that glint of sun coming off his teeth. He's the kind of guy I would have to think twice before getting the guts up to approach him or get to know. Too fake. Too plastic.

The poster, of course, is visually depicting the dangers of "beer goggles." The beer goggles that tend to slide on after drinking too much alcohol. When you are intoxicated, you begin to see people as much more attractive than they actually are. Supposedly, at least in your eyes, it turns an ugly duckling into a swan.

The sign reminds me that how I feel about my body, or my body image, can change in a short period of time. On a bad day, I feel like the ugly guy. I've put on what I call the "fear goggles." I'm afraid no one will like me and everyone will focus in on my flaws and little imperfections. An extra two pounds become twenty. My hair is frizzy and greasy. I feel repulsive and not good enough. This feeling usually hits me on the stressful days.

The "10:30 guy" is when I'm generally okay and grounded. It's the day to day, middle of the bell curve. I'm attractive enough. There are people who like me even though I'm not the person of perfection in the last picture. I feel pretty good about myself and who I am.

The midnight guy, or the way you see him when the beer goggles are on, is the person I compare myself to. It's my perfect alter ego. The way I think that I "should be." The movie star, perfect version of myself. When I hold myself up to this supermodel self, I get really down.

I try really hard to keep the beer and body goggles off. But, when they come on, due to a bad day or when I feel not good enough, I remind myself that they are just one lens through which I see myself. I am in control of taking the glasses on and off. Which means my body image is in my control.

Many or most of us probably own a pair of "body image goggles." When they are off, you look in the mirror and think "Wow, I don't look half bad." Then, out of nowhere, the tune changes. No matter what clothes you wear or how many compliments your friends give you, you just don't have a kind word to say about your own appearance. There is no talking yourself out of it.

How do you take off these body image goggles? Most books tell us to just think more positively. Love yourself. Like your body. But, believe me, we've tried that before and no it isn't quite so simple. If it were that easy, we would all be walking around feeling like Ford models. Here we will discuss the concept of "acceptance" and show how to use acceptance to create a healthy view of your body.

Beauty Is in the Eye of the Beholder

I often sing the "body image blues." The tune is all about being disappointed in my body. It sounds like the deep, sultry voice of Barry White. I've tried to silence the music by dieting. But, the song continues to play like a broken record. Wouldn't it be nice if we all had a body image tune stuck in our heads that was a little bit more like Aretha Franklin's R-E-S-P-E-C-T?

Let's start at the beginning. What exactly is a body image? Close your eyes for a second and create a mental picture of yourself. Basically, experts define body image as the *mental* picture you have of your own body and appearance—your body image is something that comes from your brain not our eyes. Notice that there's no mirror involved in this exercise.

We've all chatted with a friend who described her body as "too fat" or "too flabby" and you've thought, but not said out loud, is she crazy? When someone shares a mental picture of their body image which is wildly different from what you see with your own two eyes, it can really make you scratch your head and ask, "how can that be?" It really hits home the idea that we all see ourselves through our own "body image goggles" and not objectively.

Body Image History

Doing a body image history can help you understand how your body image, or the mental picture of yourself developed.

At age 8, I felt_____about my body. My caregivers, family, and friends would have described by my body and appearance using words like_______?

At age 12, I felt_______about my body. My caregivers described by body and appearance using words like_______________?

At age 16, _________________________________?

At age 18, _________________________________?

At my current age _____________________________?

Body Image Checkup

1. Do you check out other men's and women's bodies in a nonsexual way? In other words, do you find yourself evaluating and comparing your size and shape to that of strangers?
2. When you are in a public bathroom, are you uncomfortable standing next to someone while you are looking at yourself in the mirror?
3. Do you say critical things about yourself when you look in the mirror or are trying on clothes?
4. Do you dread summer or spring break because you'll be forced to hang out in a bathing suit?
5. Do you think your body is not thin, muscular, or defined enough?
6. Does it take you longer than a half hour to figure out what to wear?
7. Do you feel uncomfortable being naked or wearing little clothing around someone you are dating?

Don't Change!

One minute, you feel as though you could strut down the red carpet. Twenty minutes later you want to pull a sweatshirt over your head and hide in bed. How is it possible to live with the drastic ups and downs of body image?

The diet industry's magic answer to this question is if you don't love what you see 100 percent of the time, change your body! If you whittle down your figure, you will adore your body. Starve yourself. Exercise like crazy and you will fall madly, head over heals in love with your body. It's a clever trick they pulled on us. We kind of like being force-fed this formula. It makes it seem like drastically changing your body is something within your control or power. Sure, you can do little improvements. You can dress up. A new haircut does wonders. But, the reality of it is, a body is a body. It can only change so much. It will never be transformed into an entirely different body, as the dieting ads promise, without living an unrealistic and often unhealthy lifestyle.

It often takes many rounds of dieting and going broke buying useless products before we start to finally catch on that diets just don't deliver what they promise. When you try to make dramatic changes and fail, it's likely to make you feel ten times more miserable.

Botox Ads, Extreme Makeovers, and the Swan

In the past few years, there have been a seemingly endless stream of TV shows, ads, movies, and products that promote drastic measures to perfect one's appearance—no matter what the cost. "The Swan" and "Extreme Makeovers" are two examples of programming that suggest that you can replace our old body with a surgically altered and perfected one. Women featured on these two shows have endured multiple plastic surgeries, thousands of dollars worth of cosmetic dentistry, and drastic diets. Each contestant received multiple procedures like tummy tucks, botox injections, liposuction, and face lifts.

What do these shows say about the pursuit of ideal beauty? With the swipe of a credit card, your imperfections can be surgically erased and you will feel better about yourself. In this context, self-worth is limited to your outer appearance. The "ugly ducklings" on "The Swan" even competed against each other in a beauty competition to see which one had made the most dramatic transformation. The women—all self-proclaimed ugly ducklings—were competing to become the winner, "The Swan," and the prettiest and best contestant. Many of the women featured told stories about how they did not feel good about themselves because of their appearance. Did the producers think about the psychological well-being of the fragile women who did not win the competition? Will their new appearance be enough to protect their self-esteem? Will the women actually feel different about themselves when they realize that the problems that they had before their transformation did not go away just because they have new noses and larger breasts?

Can a person really change how they feel about themselves through plastic surgery as "The Swan" suggests? It's like wrapping the same birthday present in a different colored paper. Packaging can only help so much. Once opened, the gift inside is the same no matter what the outside wrapping looks like. Cosmetic changes will not change one's personality. A rude person with a new nose job will still be a rude person. It is true that improving your appearance may make you more attractive. Many of the women admitted that they felt better about their appearance. But, the surgeries do not perform a metamorphosis to the part of the brain that has felt less than perfect or unacceptable for so many years.

Sure, we like to think that some people really are "perfect," like the models in glamour magazines. We are well aware that these images are airbrushed. Cindy Crawford, a supermodel, was once quoted as saying that she didn't even look as good as Cindy Crawford. In real life, she doesn't measure up to her airbrushed twin. Her computer altered image was airbrushed to remove every blemish, wrinkle, and pore. Although we know that the photographs of models in magazines are airbrushed to produce a perfect look, people often forget or ignore that information when viewing the finished product. We tuck that information below our awareness. Despite knowledge that these photographs are unrealistic images, people still try to attain their impossible ideal of beauty.

Barbie Gone Wild

Barbie and her friends have taken the most heat in debates about the epidemic of body loathing. Could the twelve-inch plastic Barbie, the most popular doll in America, really cause eating problems? Barbie is the stereotypic, perfect all-American beauty, blonde and blue eyed.

She is "perfect." Parents and body image experts question the influence that "perfect" dolls have upon young girls. Clearly, most girls will grow up to look nothing like Barbie. Will girls compare themselves to her? Do they want to be like her? Will Barbie be their first role model? It's hard to say what kind of power she may have. However, there is one case that has been well-documented by the media of a woman who has spent thousands of dollars to have over a dozen surgeries to make herself into a real Barbie.

Barbie isn't responsible for all the eating disorders and dieters in America. Barbie is merely a doll that is one piece of a very complex puzzle. Many other dolls, TV shows, and magazines convey the exact same message. Barbie is a symbol that represents all the reasons why so many people struggle with body image dissatisfaction. Just like a flag and other symbolic objects, she is the item we hold up in the air to summarize the cultural factors contributing to body image problems across the nation.

So, what does Barbie stand for? Barbie perpetuates the *idea* that beauty, thinness and perfection are important. Barbie is all about how she looks, what she wears and what kind of cool car she drives. You do her hair and dress her up and that's about it. The play is focused on image and appearance. Efforts have been made to give her a personality by giving her respectable occupations like doctor, veterinarian, teacher, and soldier. But she still looks exactly the same—pink heels and flowing blond hair. We don't know who Barbie is as a person. To us, she is plastic, stiff, beautiful, and always smiling. Her image lacks the ethnic diversity, intelligence, and emotional richness of the women she represents.

Lots of little girls love their Barbies dearly and never give a second thought to her symbolic role in life. There is another group of kids who are vulnerable to any messages about perfection and body image. Does early exposure to images of perfection and the importance of beauty plant a damaging seed in some children's heads? Will those seeds bloom long after girls have stopped playing with their Barbie?

Academic Barbie

In the past few years, several universities and organizations have built life-size Barbies to symbolize the media's absurd emphasis on perfection. If she were a real person, a life-size Barbie would be much taller than any supermodel we know of (seven feet tall), have a breast size bigger than Marilyn Monroe, and a waist smaller than a twelve-year-old child. Clearly, she would be just a little bit freakish. The life-size Barbie has been known to frequent campus parties and visit wellness weeks to do her symbolic duty.

> If you want to learn more about Barbie's influence on the world, check out www.audiosbarbie.com. It's a great Web site for women and girls of "every body" size and shape. Find out the scandalous secrets of Barbie's past.

What Can We Do?

Unfortunately, unrealistically thin models and sexualized images probably aren't going away soon. The best case scenario is that the advertising agencies themselves begin to move away from dangerously thin models and their focus on emaciated men and women. There are some wonderful glimmers of hope and evidence of this happening. A few major companies are using models of various shapes, sizes, and ethnic backgrounds to represent the pantheon of beautiful women and men.

But, until the rest of the advertisers follow suit, what can you do? The enormous size of the media industry can feel incredibly overwhelming. Joining a media watchdog organization can make you feel and be more active. These groups ask consumers to keep an eye out for offensive, degrading, or damaging ads and commercials. The organization sends letters and holds advertisers accountable for the messages they put on billboards and in magazine spreads (see www.nationaleatingdisorders.org and www.cswd.org).

Joining an organization is a great start. But, what can you do while flipping through a glamour magazine when you catch a glimpse of a supermodel without an ounce of fat in a bikini? Studies show that even a brief exposure to a magazine ad can have a negative impact on mood and increase body image dissatisfaction (Tiggemann and McGill 2004).

One piece of advice is to simply observe your reaction. Often, we see these ads without thinking much about them. We flip quickly by the advertisements but the split second is enough for you to mindlessly absorb their messages. Instead of looking at these ads with a detached awareness, consider what effect they have on you and others. Think about the true purpose of these ads and the reasons why a particular model has been selected to represent a product. Advertisers want you to think that in order to look like this model you must buy this brand of perfume. They want you to believe that you cannot achieve their ideal of beauty or thinness without buying their product.

> About-Face (www.about-face.org) promotes positive self-esteem in girls and women of all ages, sizes, races, and backgrounds through a spirited approach to media education, outreach, and activism.

The Six-Pack Abs Dilemma

Once upon a time, we believed women were the only people anxiously looking in the mirror and fretting about their figure. Then came well-dressed hunks in *GQ* and *Men's Health* outlining diet tricks, half-naked Calvin Klein underwear models, rock-hard abs selling colognes, and Abercrombie and Fitch models with nearly flawless bodies. Clearly, these things hit home the message that looks matter more and more even for men.

Just like their female counterparts, the media would like men to believe that if they just diet right and workout like crazy, they too can magically transform their body into a cut, amazing physique. These messages try to say that the average Joe, with enough hard work, can whip himself into the same shape as a male model. We know, of course, this is far from the truth. Your actual body and "your ideal body" don't always have the potential to coincide, no matter how hard you work. The push for men to worry about their appearance has definitely raised men's anxiety. Between 9 and 12 percent of men, in one study, reported being unhappy with their body shape, felt fat, and seriously wanted to lose weight (O'Dea et al. 2002).

Men have it rough. They worry about being overweight and fear that they are too thin. On top of that, they also worry about their shape and size. The "ideal body" for men includes elements of a masculine physique (V-shaped), tallness, and a muscular body. We have all heard the put downs and taunts men use among themselves, which further perpetuate the problem ("wimp," "sissy"). These labels emphasize the social pressure to have a strong, muscular body.

Many men feel pushed to live up to this standard. Some are willing to take it to extremes. For example, there are a number of plastic surgery options for men to help them achieve this ideal, such as pectoral and calf implants. Not to mention a litany of dangerous synthetic drugs to pump up the body to unnatural proportions, and fad dieting to slim it down. Clearly, men are also caving under the pressure to live up to unrealistic body expectations.

Sex and Body Image

Picture this scene. You just snagged an attractive individual you've been eyeing at the fraternity party all night. He asks to walk you to your dorm. When you arrive at the door, you both lean in and kiss. His hand travels to your waist and begins to caress your stomach. You suddenly become very uncomfortable. You stop. It isn't his hands you mind or are thinking about, it's your stomach. You cringe at the mere thought of him touching the little bulge that you hate and wish you could erase. He feels your discomfort and stops.

Or, how about this: you are making out with your new girlfriend. You are in the middle of a passionate make-out session. She goes to pull off your t-shirt. But, you maneuver away. You try to redirect her attention. She backs off just long enough for you to turn down the lights for some romantic lighting. But, your smooth move isn't about giving your dingy apartment a little ambiance. You don't want her to see your puny body. Her past boyfriend was like Arnold Schwarzenegger. You imagine she is going to die laughing. Or worse, walk out. You continue to feel awkward despite the low lights. As you pull away, you can see in her eyes that she feels rejected.

A poor body image is a significant road block to a healthy intimate life. Feeling good about yourself comes way before you can genuinely be with someone else mentally or physically. Feeling uncomfortable with your body can be a huge obstruction. The good news is that a large portion of it boils down to your own attitude. None of us has to feel like a diva or a stud to accept that our body should be protected and treated kindly. We all deserve to be treated with respect, and if you show reverence for your body, it's more likely that your significant other will too.

> Check out: http://www.smartersex.org. It's a good place to gather information to help in defining your own sexual/intimacy boundaries. This book respects the sexual choices of all its readers whether they choose abstinence or practice safe intimacy/sex. When choosing to be intimate, please do so responsibly and mindfully.

The Danger

Body image problems should not be taken lightly. Studies show that a poor body image can lead to emotional distress, low self-esteem, dieting, anxiety, depression, and particularly eating disorders. Let's say

Alex has a poor body image. She feels pretty bad about herself overall. She goes on a diet hoping that losing ten pounds will make her feel better. After two months, she drops ten pounds, which momentarily makes her feel pretty proud of herself. She gets a lot of compliments. But, her weight loss high fades quickly and the admiration dies down once people get used to the change.

Nothing else in her life has changed. Her problems are still lingering. She still is unhappy with her controlling mother and the weight loss wasn't exactly a dragnet for dates as she had hoped. She wants the high she got from the weight loss back! So, she decides to go on another diet. When she gets to her goal weight, it's not enough. It doesn't feel different. This example shows why body image problems plus dieting can make people at significant risk for an eating problem. There are lots of factors that increase your vulnerability to really disliking your body, and teasing is one of them.

Teasing

> *In the fifth grade, Brian noticed way before I did that I was, for the lack of a better phrase, blossoming into a woman. "Hey meatballs," he yelled across the playground as he grabbed two fistfuls of his shirt and pulled it away from his chest. His comment was obviously pointing out that I was rounding out all over the place. In that moment, I transformed from an opaque knee socked girl to a woman seeking camouflaging clothes. I became acutely aware that my body was on full display for others to see, and even worse, was open to evaluation.*

Nothing is more damaging to body image than teasing. Most of us can easily recall a time when we've been teased. Seventy percent of college women report that they have been teased and that teasing affected how they experienced their body image (Cash 1995). My clients over the years have talked about a specific critical comment someone made about their body. They have said things like "in the sixth grade, my mom said I was chubby." Or a friend gave them demeaning nickname like "Kelly the jelly belly." Like the story above, it shifts the person's *awareness* to their body in a negative way. Words, even in jesting words, pollute a person's body image like acid rain eroding a sheet of metal.

The Mindless Teasing Trap

Teasing sometimes creates what I call a mindlessness trap. To change your body image, you must escape the trap. Let's say for example that someone calls a young man a "fat Albert." Understandably, he takes this cruel label to heart. "I am fat Albert," he says to himself. "Fat, disgusting and ugly Albert." By agreeing with the label, he's jumped head first into a box. He may even tell other people that he is "fat Albert." By doing this he is shutting that box and taping close the lid. He has trapped himself into thinking and treating himself in this way. His behavior starts to match the label. For example, he may avoid asking women out on dates because nobody wants to date a "fat Albert."

To begin to deal with this problem, it's important for you to bring any memories of teasing into your awareness, rather than burying them. Consider how it made you feel, thinking particularly of the part of the body that was the target of the teasing. Did the football players in high school call out "thunder thighs" when you wore your cheerleading uniform? Think about the source of the comments and the possible reasons for them. Was the teasing to motivate weight loss, was it out of jealousy, or just mean spirited? Does the teaser have his or her own weight or body image issue? And remember, never tease others.

What Is Body Image Acceptance?

Miss Piggy, the Muppet, is the queen of self-acceptance. She is quite a voluptuous pig who exudes radical, or complete, "self-acceptance." Her self-confidence obviously is not based on having a thin figure. Instead, she accepts her figure and pampers her body. Miss Piggy is always dressed up in low cut, form fitting gowns and furs. She simply feels beautiful and expects the world to treat her as if she is the most gorgeous and desirable pig in the world. If someone dares to snicker about her weight, she gives them a solid karate chop. Wouldn't it be nice to have this kind of radical self-acceptance?

A mindful approach to creating a healthy body image is based on the notion of "acceptance." It doesn't mean loving and adoring one's body. For many of us, that simply wouldn't be true. So, it's not about lying to yourself or trying to talk yourself into something that you don't believe. Acceptance is a comfortable middle ground between disliking and loving your body. It is a more realistic approach.

There is nothing magical about "acceptance." It is simply a way of uncritical observation. Nonjudgmental observations help you appreciate the many ways in which our body serves you. For example, you may notice and appreciate that you can breathe and walk, have pretty finger nails, and naturally curly hair—not to mention that your shape has some redeeming qualities. You may not have Rockette legs, but then again your legs are pretty good assets on the soccer field. It's a question of recognizing that it's not *all* bad. Rather than placing a value judgment on your body as "good" or "bad," you can more usefully take a more neutral stance and tell yourself that "it is what it is." No matter how much you may dislike your body, it's all yours, and the more you fight it, the unhappier you get.

Think about acceptance this way. Let's say you have lower back pain that really hurts and makes it very hard to sit. This is a ripe opportunity to get stuck in a pity party. Poor me, it hurts. You may become bitter because you never used to have back pain, and you get deeper and deeper into resenting that you even have to deal with it. You can get stuck in this "poor me" mode for a very long time. Eventually, you arrive at a place of acceptance and say to yourself, "Okay, so I have back pain. It's not fun, but it's okay, now what do I do? How can I work to make it better?" Once you have accepted it, you move on to find ways to cope with it like focusing on relaxation exercises, physical therapy, and pain management. Like the back pain example, you can get in a rut about feeling unhappy and resentful about weight problems. You get so stuck in not accepting the problem, that you can't find ways to deal with it.

Greetings,
I'm writing you this letter because I think it is about time I tell you how I truly feel. It's hard for me to say what I have to say because I feel guilty. I know you didn't choose me to be yours and it's not like you could give me back. However, we are related to each other and for that reason you will always be part of me and I will always be a part of you. We are pretty much joined at the hip forever.

For the most part, I never felt good enough for you. Sure, I wasn't perfect, but who is? You always made critical comments about me. Once, you even said that you hated me. I felt ashamed and unappreciated.

It wasn't all bad. I did appreciate when you cared for and nurtured me. You tried to protect me and keep me warm. If I was injured, you were always there to make sure I was okay. There were some days you actually seemed to look at me in an accepting way. Your smile and approving nod make me stronger and happy.

The least you could do is acknowledge what an important and vital part I've been in your life. I was there through everything. I walked you through every important event in your life. Preschool through graduation. Can you imagine life without me? What would it be like trying to stand on your own? Who would take you where you want to go? Who would play and walk with you? From now on, I just ask for your unconditional love and support. You don't have to try to hide me anymore or be ashamed of me. Most of all, please just accept me and love me for what I am.

—Love, Your Left Thigh

In this client's letter to herself, you can hear that self-acceptance is a process. Your ability to accept yourself may come and go, but that's okay, acceptance takes time.

Body Mindfulness Homework

Try a mirror exercise. This means standing in front of the mirror for an extended length of time. Your task is simply to describe yourself without using judgmental language (no words like *fat*, *ugly*, or *stupid*). First, describe your hair (including the color, length, and texture). Notice the shape of your legs and your shoulders. Describe your silhouette. Then, put into words some of the important functions that some of your body parts play in your role as a college student. Perhaps your fist helps you to play volleyball or your hip allows you to balance your grocery bags and books. Use the letter above to get into the perspective of the body part. Just use neutral adjectives. Remember, you are coming to a place of acceptance.

Skinny Is in the Eye of the Beholder

Another way to build self-acceptance is to stop comparing yourself to everyone around you. In college, students will write many papers comparing and contrasting books, literature, and research. It's no surprise that this would also happen, consciously or subconsciously, with your body. Am I as pretty? Who is thinner, me or her? How do I compare to my roommate? Some colleges even foster a competitive environment. Grade curves, leadership awards, and cut throat competition for a select number of jobs push people to be "better" than their classmates in every way possible.

When you appreciate how much *context* affects body image, it's easy to understand why it isn't helpful to compare yourself to anyone else. Imagine how it would feel to walk into a room where everyone is ten pounds thinner than you are. Now, imagine walking into that same room and you are ten pounds lighter than all the other people milling around the room. Your weight never changed but how you felt about yourself would probably be drastically different in each scenario. Here is another example. Let's say you finally get assigned to live in a single apartment. You are thrilled by your good fortune. No more roommates. Your enthusiasm fades after you visit a friend who got a deluxe suite apartment. You weren't the least bit unhappy with your apartment until you saw hers.

Who do you measure yourself up against? Do you have a self-image twin? Maybe you compare yourself to a former image of yourself ("When I was twelve, I was a twig and now I'm much heavier). Or, maybe your standard of measure is your best friend (she is so much prettier than I am) or a celebrity. Instead of comparing, think about your own potential.

Getting to Acceptance

Working on acceptance isn't easy. Eighteen plus years of dieting and disliking your body isn't going to magically change overnight. It takes practice. Below are affirmations to help in getting started. Hang them up on the bathroom mirror. Post them on the door, on the bulletin board in the dorm hallway, or inside the bathroom stall door. Let them soak in and marinate in your brain.

Acceptance Affirmations

- I *accept* that my eating and weight concerns are creating emotional distress, discomfort, and suffering in my life. These concerns distract from my ability to be a student, focus on my education, and to be happy.
- I *accept* that I am my own standard of measure. Comparing myself to my friends and classmates is futile and only leads to my own unhappiness.
- I *accept* that my body cannot be given a grade like homework.

- I choose to *accept* my body and weight as they are at this moment. I won't get stuck in regretting the past or dreaming about the future. I will think about who I am in this moment.
- Committing to *accept* myself is a choice only I can make. I won't do it for my significant other, my parents or my friends.
- I *accept* that my genetic inheritance strongly influences my body shape and weight.
- I *accept* how important it is for me to eat mindfully in order to live a healthy life. I need to eat mindfully to power my brain to study to the best of my ability, have the power to play sports, and the energy to meet my potential.
- To *accept* my body and weight does not mean that I am judging them to be perfect. I recognize that the college environment fosters high expectations and pressure to compete.
- *Acceptance* only comes from within myself. My grades and words of praise from others are external not internal sources of validation.
- I *accept* that my worth is not reflected by my weight and shape, but rather, my worth is determined by who I am as a whole person. My self-esteem comes from participating in campus groups, working hard, living in accordance with my values, being a true friend, and using my talents wisely.
- *Acceptance* includes rejecting the cultural and social messages I receive about weight. I am mindful of the effect of TV, magazines, and movie stars and seek realistic and healthy role models.

Chapter 6, Mindful Eating 101: When you "accept" your body, you are okay with who you are in this very moment. Acceptance is a neutral stance. You don't love your reflection nor do you hate your appearance. There is no judgment or stamp of approval placed upon yourself. Acceptance requires no change to your body or weight.

Chapter 7:

Supersizing

Sizing Up Self-Esteem

For my psychology class, our assignment was to imagine that you won the state lottery. For the prize, you could either choose a brand new, red convertible BMW and a few hundred thousand dollars or high self-esteem and confidence for life. Each student had to write and essay about which one he or she would choose and why. That was a tough one. I feel pretty good about myself, but I pictured how my life would change if I had rock solid self-esteem. It would do wonders for my academic success and career. I could finally get the guts to ask someone out. It really made me pause to think.

I started to ask my friends, which prize would you choose? I figured that if a person already had high self-esteem, they would clearly take the money, and if not, the high self-esteem over the cash seemed like a smarter choice. With an intact self-esteem you would know that if you wanted a fancy sports car or money, you would believe right down to your core that you would make it happen. You'd be confident that you could reach all of your goals. In fact, you might not even need material things to be happy. Your sense of security and well-being would come from within.

Self-esteem is priceless, something we all want, but one of those things money just can't buy. If only someone could package it up and market it, he or she would be a very rich person. Oh, wait a minute. Someone has tried to market it: It's called dieting products.

Dieting and Self-Esteem: The "If Only" Syndrome

"If only I could lose five pounds, then I would feel good about myself!"
—Amy

Weight loss and dieting products are marketed as the magic answer to fixing low or shaky self-esteem. The diet industry loves people who seek better self-esteem and preys on them like vultures. The industry has them right where it wants them. People who lack confidence are desperate for a quick fix, not to mention are willing to buy and pay just about anything. It's a CEO's dream come true—the perfect target market.

One of my clients bought a bucket sized portion of protein drink mix, which tasted like a mixture of peas and ketchup, because it promised that she'd lose five pounds in a week. She did lose five pounds but not from her body. She threw away the five-gallon container that cost her fifty dollars. Feeling stupid for wasting her money and failing at this attempt were further blows to her self-esteem. Another client actually bought a shock collar so that she could zap herself when she was about to eat a dessert. Ironically, this product was bought with the hope that it would bring her a step closer to feeling better about herself. However, it was humiliating. She was embarrassed that she would go to this length to lose weight. This made her feel desperate and naïve for trying such a worthless product.

The real answer to patching up self-esteem doesn't cost a thing. It's about acceptance. When you lack self-acceptance, you walk around with the belief that you need to be "fixed" and that you aren't okay exactly as you are. Sure, we can all make little improvements to ourselves. But, what I'm talking about is the feeling of "I am an unacceptable human being who needs a complete personality and body adjustment."

Single, twenty-something, college student in search of real self.
Seeking empowerment, success, and a strong voice.
Authenticity and honesty a strong plus.

Must love a natural, healthy and strong body.
Desires positive self-esteem, genuine relationships,
and total self-acceptance.

Do You Really Need Self-Esteem?

Yes, indeed you do. Self-esteem is like the immune system, it isn't visible, but it's there all the same, and it is there to protect you. People with strong self-esteem take care of themselves and act in accordance with their conscience. They respect themselves. Self-esteem also helps you bounce back from disappointments and mistakes. People with a low self-esteem continue to beat themselves a long time after they have made an error. Self-esteem braces you to withstand insults and criticism and still know that you are okay no matter what happens. During times of stress in particular, you need self-esteem to help you to keep going rather than crumpling up in a corner and hiding.

A lot of people think that having a positive view of yourself, or high self-esteem, is something that you will "feel" or will magically fix their problems. It's not that dramatic—it's not a thunderboltlike feeling. There may be certain areas of one's life in which you have a stronger or weaker feeling of self-esteem. For example, perhaps academically a person may feel pretty confident but be less sure in relationships. Another misperception about self-esteem is that it will come across as conceited. Self-esteem does not mean judging yourself to be the best and greatest person in the world. It is a middle ground between grandiosity and feeling unworthy. In this state, you are respectful, okay with who you are, and feel deserving.

Self-Esteem and Sexiness

Attractive people, those with movie star good looks, are often assumed to have high self-esteem. Take a look at Princess Diana. She was considered one of the most photographed and beautiful women in the world. However, before her death, she openly spoke about her very low self-esteem. And low self-esteem was one aspect of her life that was speculated to have prompted several suicide attempts, bulimia, and severe unhappiness.

We often wonder how movie stars and even stunningly attractive people who are not famous can develop low self-esteem when from the outside they appear to have everything they could ever want? The answer is pretty simple: They are human. Self-esteem is an internal mechanism, not an external one, which is lodged deep in your brain, and it really can't see what you look like. So, your self-esteem isn't impressed with thinness, money, fame, or beauty. It's a feeling inside that truly believes you are okay no matter what anyone else says.

Self-Esteem and Eating Issues

There seems to be a significant connection between self-esteem and problematic eating. Positive self-esteem can actually be a "protective factor" against the development of an eating disorder (Cervera, Lahortiga, Martinez-Gonzalez, Gual, and Irala-Estevez 2003). It makes sense. If you already have high self-esteem, you don't need to find ways to fix it, so turning to dieting would be less likely.

A Self-Esteem Nightmare

On a scale of one to ten, my self-esteem was about a two. When I didn't think it could get any lower, it fell to minus one. I started dating Brian during my sophomore year. Brian is an attractive senior guy living on the third floor of my dorm. Some people call it "dormcest" like incest because we lived in the same building and that is a little close for comfort. Women swooned at the mere mention of his name. One of my hall mates had his schedule plotted out on her PDA.

The "only" problem was that Brian had been dating a woman in my physics class for about three years. Despite his girl friend, Brian and I were all over each other. We had sex everywhere. We did it behind book stacks in the library, on the quad at night, and in the communal showers. We'd hook up often, but we'd never set foot out of my dorm room nor did we go out on a real date. At first, I didn't really care. I got these temporary boosts to my self-esteem. I felt wanted, which meant I must be "okay."

One night, he invited me to a hot tub party at his fraternity house. At one point, it was just Brian, myself, and his roommate in the hot tub. We were drinking in the steamy tub. First, he said he wanted me to skinny dip. I self-consciously stripped off my bikini. I tried to act sexy and do my best strip tease. The alcohol and my low self-esteem were a lethal combination and unfortunately probably would have made me say yes to just about anything. He somehow talked me into hooking up with both of them in the hot tub. He told me he thought it would be pretty hot. I didn't want to lose him.

The next day he dumped me over the Internet. He started with a cryptic "away" message and then sent me a nasty text message. The final straw was being completely kicked off his "buddy list." Brian claimed he was angry I hooked up with someone else. This rejection destroyed any crumbs of self-esteem I had left. The next day, I wrote "stupid" on the inner palm of my hand in blue pen. I guess it was a reminder and punishment for what I did.

I yearned for that magic wand to bop me on the top of the head and fix my self-esteem. I envied other women who seemed to effortlessly have the self-confidence, self-respect, and self-love that I yearned for. Realistically, I knew it wasn't going to magically change. My magic wand came more in the form of a ballpoint pen. I wrote down things to keep reminding myself that I was okay. This time feeling good had to come from the inside rather than seeking someone else to help me raise it.

An obvious red flag indicating low self-esteem is when you do things that are disrespectful to yourself. Maybe it is acting in a way that goes against the grain of your value system. Or, you get a gut sense that something isn't right. As in the story above, it could be allowing someone to take advantage of your low self-esteem or vulnerability.

Unfortunately, the effects of low self-esteem are too often witnessed or most obvious in romantic relationships. A person with a low self-esteem allows (or doesn't even realize) that someone else is harming their body sexually or emotionally beating them up like a punching bag. The disrespect happens, in part, because they don't believe that they deserve anything better, they don't think anyone else will want them or that if they were more attractive than they could date someone more respectful. Take a closer look at your relationships and consider whether they are a boost or detriment to how you feel about yourself.

Four Masks of Low Self-Esteem

The Fraud: This person appears to the world as if they have a healthy self-esteem. However, they are always worried that someone will find out that they aren't as confident as they seem and don't have it all together.

The "I Don't Care": This person comes across as if they don't care or worry about what other people think. Sometimes they purposefully do things that they know others will dislike to prove that they don't concern themselves with other people's opinions. However, in reality, they spend a lot of time worrying about what others think.

The "I'm Not Worth It": This person clearly lets other people know that they do not have high self-esteem. They may criticize themselves openly or treat themselves poorly because they feel that is what they deserve.

The "I'm Great": This person tells friends and family all about their greatness and achievements. Their public declaration of how wonderful they are really covers an insecure self. This attitude is a self defense against really feeling low self-esteem to its fullest.

Contributors to Low Self-Esteem

Why do some people seem to have self-esteem and others don't? Self-esteem is built like a brick wall. Your parents or primary caregivers begin building the wall when you are born. Their main job is to build a strong foundation. Parents construct the wall with praise, listening, validating your feelings, and most important, by separating your bad behavior from being a bad person. If your parents don't have strong self-esteem themselves, it's difficult for them to build a solid one for their children. A weak self-esteem is like a foundation resting on sand. It's easy to crumble, sinks from time to time, and is in need of constant external reinforcement.

Although your parents build the foundation, there are a lot of other things that affect the building of the wall from that time on. Bricks are constantly added to this wall. When someone compliments you, another brick is added. An accomplishment makes the wall more solid. When a healthy self-esteem exists, there is not the need for praise or validation from other people because you have a strong foundation and you can give yourself a pat on the back.

The self-esteem wall protects you from hurtful experiences. When you have a setback, disappointment, or criticism, it doesn't knock you down. A grade of D– on a chemistry midterm will lead you to remind yourself that you can try again, rather than saying "There is no way I can do this, I might as well drop out." Someone with low self-esteem will constantly need compliments to hold them together or keep them from beating themselves up emotionally.

Negative self-talk, sexual abuse, and perfectionism are like rocks thrown at the wall that break it down bit by bit.

Negative Self-Talk

Many of us talk to ourselves in a very negative way and evaluate ourselves as being of little worth. We throw insults at ourselves and say things that can't help but drag down our self-esteem. They are judgmental statements that often don't separate the act from the person. For example, it's one thing to mindlessly overeat but another thing to tell oneself that one's a stupid idiot for doing so. To do this is to judge the act and the worth of the person as being the same. Instead, see chapter 9 to learn how to speak more mindfully.

Past Sexual Abuse or Sexual Assault

Sadly, date rape and sexual assault are a tragic reality for many men and women on college campuses. The emotional and physical scars of assault can deeply wound one's body and self-esteem. Shame, body hate, anger, and embarrassment are just a few words to describe the devastating psychological effects of sexual assault and rape.

When bad things happen to your body, signs of distress may take a physical form. Sometimes this can result in focusing on eating, disliking your body, or feeling bad about yourself. It is an unconscious way of expressing that something bad happened to your body. People with a negative body image usually feel uncomfortable and lack confidence about their body. In part, this explains the connection between sexual abuse/assault, self-esteem, and eating problems. Anyone who has been assaulted in any way should talk to a trusted professional to gain help healing. See appendix A at the back of this book for information on how to find a counselor.

Failure and Accomplishments

People often don't think too much about their self-esteem, until something threatens it. For example, flunking a test might make you label yourself as "dumb" or question your intelligence. Until that moment, your intelligence level didn't come into question. Setbacks and errors can really make you ponder your self-esteem.

We often try to raise self-esteem through accomplishments or by doing things that will get praise and recognition, such as getting good grades. This is earned self-esteem. Another way to raise self-esteem is through developing a sense of competency over a certain area of your life. Self-esteem comes from doing the things you truly love and working hard at it. The process, what you're doing and how much you are getting out of it, is just as important as the outcome. Too often, we focus on the end result as the accomplishment-winning or losing. Success is not a bad thing. However, it can be risky to pin one's worth on just the outcome. Let's say you feel good about yourself because you get straight As. What if there's a particularly tough professor in a class you don't like? Or, what if you get mono and miss a lot of classes? Giving something a try is also worthy of praise and can be an accomplishment. Say you never ran a marathon before. It doesn't matter if you finish or not, if you enjoyed the training process.

Perfectionism

When you meet a perfectionist, you often know it immediately. They reek with dissatisfaction about themselves. Even an "A" doesn't feel good enough because it isn't an "A plus." Perfectionists struggle with self-esteem because they can never reach this impossible state of flawlessness. No such perfection exists. It's a setup to one's self-esteem. Perfectionists just never feel "good enough."

On the positive side, perfectionists work very hard and are successful. They are star athletes and valedictorians. Perfectionists expend a lot of effort. They put 110 percent into everything they do. For example, they may proofread a term paper repeatedly. Sometimes they are proofreading the paper until the very moment they have to turn it in to their professor. Rechecking their work is a benefit to their academic performance. Teachers like perfectionists because they do stellar work. Classmates want them for group projects because they will get the job done and often put in the most effort.

The desire for perfection, however, can be crippling. One of my clients refused to hand in a completed ten-page paper because she felt it wasn't "good enough." She obtained a zero for simply not turning it in. Perfectionism is also frustrating to relationships. The partner of a perfectionist often has the impression that they are not good enough. They feel pressured to meet the perfectionist's expectations about how to dress or act. The partner either lives up to the expectation or decides that he or she cannot be in the relationship.

If you are a perfectionist, it is important to accept that you are "human." As humans, we all make mistakes, have imperfections and weaknesses. It is quite natural. A mistake doesn't always signify a shortcoming. It's important to work on accepting who you are rather than who you think you "should be."

Self-acceptance for perfectionists also means setting realistic expectations for yourself. Let's take the example of mindful eating. A perfectionist would feel that mindful eating must be mastered right "now." In fact, it should have been done yesterday. Maybe a perfectionist would even judge him- or herself for not being a "good enough mindful eater."

To overcome the limitations of perfectionism, a person would first need to adopt a nonjudgmental attitude. This means appreciating his or her body, focusing on his or her assets, and using positive language. A perfectionist's challenge would be to accept that learning mindful eating skills is a process and a journey.

Signs of a Perfectionist

- Holds the irrational belief that he or she cannot make a mistake
- Hyperalert to imperfections, slipups, or errors
- Strives to be the best or "on top"
- Focuses on the way things are "supposed to be" and uses the word *should* a lot
- Only approaches challenges that he or she can master or perfect
- Never feels "good enough"
- Desires to "win" at everything
- Always feels behind and as if he or she should have more done
- Holds high expectations for self and others
- Uses the word *perfect* a lot to describe things and events
- Expends a lot of energy looking for just the right item
- "Filters" out positive information; instead of seeing a completed and well-researched thirty-page paper as an accomplishment, he or she is disturbed that the title page isn't perfectly centered

Mindfulness Homework

One of the best ways to raise your self-esteem is to seek the help and perspective of important people in your life. However, I say this with an important aside. Seek the help of *emotionally healthy and supportive people.*

How Do I Love Me? Let Me Count the Ways

The worst case scenario is that you find another person with equally low self-esteem or worse. Caregivers can be a great support. However, often, they often can be one contributor to a faulty self-esteem foundation or have unrealistic expectations of us. Talking to friends, professors, and acquaintances will help you develop a well rounded and unbiased view of yourself.

The next thing is to really listen to what friends and family have to say. Often, the compliments and feedback we get from others falls on deaf ears. Do you turn down compliments or get defensive when someone offers some helpful feedback? Praise is what lets us know that we are accepted and appreciated. When we listen to other people's praise, we internalize it and it teaches us how to praise ourselves. It helps you pinpoint your true talents and value.

How to Mindfully Raise Self-Esteem

The following are some self-esteem spritzers:

Aware: To be more aware of your self-esteem highs and lows, write a self-esteem autobiography. Start by drawing a time line, plotting out some moments throughout life where you felt really good about yourself. List the age, event, and how you felt. Notice what increases your self-esteem. Is it academic grades, awards, a relationship, a comment from a friend or parent? Also note what causes dips in self-esteem. Write about the thoughts and events that were helpful in dealing with particularly low moments.

Observe: Rank order these dimension of self-esteem (academic performance, relationships, friendship, health, personality, job success, sports, health, family, spiritual, accomplishments). Be mindful of the area where self-esteem is highest and those that may need a little more attention.

Looking at the gray areas: Create realistic expectations. We often set our standards so high that we can't possibly reach them. Many students have such lofty, long-term goals (buying a house, being a CEO) that they can't feel the pleasure that comes with reaching a day-to-day goal like doing well on a test. Or, sometimes the goals are set way too low so that it doesn't require much effort to reach them. When that is the case, crossing the finish line of these easy goals doesn't serve to build a more solid self-esteem. The trick is setting long- and short-term goals that are just within reach.

Shift out of autopilot: If you find that the same old strategies for dealing with self-esteem issues aren't working, new tools are called for. A good source of information on self-esteem is to be found in the following books: *Self-Esteem: A Proven Program of Cognitive Techniques for Assessing, Improving, and Maintaining Your Self-Esteem* by Matthew McKay and Patrick Fanning; *The Body Image Workbook* by Thomas F. Cash; *Self-Esteem: Tools For Recovery,* by Lindsay Hall and Leigh Cohen; *Weight Wisdom: Affirmations to Free You From Food and Body Concerns*, by Kathleen Burns Kingsbury and Mary Ellen Williams.

Being in the moment: Visualize the confident *you.* Simply using one's imagination is a surprisingly powerful tool. You can't get what you want if you can't see it. So, imagine for a moment that you have the confidence you want. How would you know that your self-esteem had improved? Describe the behaviors that would be different. Consider what you can do in this moment to act in accordance with that vision. You can spend more time doing useful things to improve yourself and less time sitting and dwelling on what you don't have.

Nonjudgment: Create your own self-esteem mantra. Repeat the mantra to yourself whenever you notice the critical inner self kicking in. Write yourself text messages and fill Post-It notes with positive self-statements. Find nonjudgmental and compassionate quotes that encourage you. Try www.quotationspage.com.

Acceptance: Healthy self-esteem means becoming aware of your personal strengths and accepting yourself as a worthy person despite any real limitations. Make a top ten list of things you want to work on "accepting" about yourself.

> ***Chapter 7, Mindful Eating 101:*** Dieting products, fashion magazines, and the "pressure to be thin" loom over you and serve as constant threats to self-esteem. The media also tries persistently to convince you that self-esteem can be fixed through transforming your appearance. Self-esteem comes from accepting yourself as you are. You can change how you view yourself, without changing your body or your personality. Be mindful of how you respect yourself and think nonjudgmentally. This frame of mind does wonders for self-esteem.

Chapter 8

Swallowing Feelings

Food and Emotion

I graduated from college two years ago. Since then, I've experienced a variety of recurring dreams, which could actually qualify as nightmares. In one version, someone calls me to tell me I have to return to college because I didn't have the required credits to graduate. To pass, I have to retake the final cumulative chemistry exam again to get these credits. I find myself in a classroom, blue book in hand, staring at a thirty-page final exam. The test isn't even multiple choice. It's all essay. Of course, I've missed all of the classes, so I don't know the answers to any of the questions. I scan the classroom and see that my peers are working diligently and seem to breeze through it. I feel myself begin to panic. My heart pounds, I'm dripping with sweat, and I try to leave the classroom. However, the teacher won't allow me to leave without turning in the exam. I wake up in a cold sweat.

College Is the Best Time of Your Life

True, college can be a blast, but, like anything it has its ups and downs. This adage most often comes out of the mouths of alumni or parents who haven't set foot in a classroom for many years. Students have heard their nostalgic sighs, seen their faraway looks, and references to college as a nirvana-like place. They've forgotten about the day to day stress and some of the very significant challenges and difficult life decisions. Where is this ideal place alumni talk about where there are few responsibilities and virtually no worries?

The idealization of college perpetuates the myth that higher education is a wondrous paradise and truly perfect. Everyone is happy. Everyone is partying. This simply isn't true. Students sometimes feel that if they aren't having a good time something is wrong with them. They fear that they have missed something that everyone else had access to. If every waking hour isn't a party or a rip roaring good time, that's okay. It's not meant to be.

Not All Stress Is Bad (Really)

> *Stress, to me, is like a game of Jenga, a simple game in which you build a tower of blocks. Then you pull one of the blocks out of the middle of the tower and put it on top. The goal is to avoid being the loser who knocks it over. My strategy is to tap and poke each piece lightly to see if it will come out easily. I see all the stresses in my life like the blocks. Sometimes I'm poking at my class schedule and think, wow, that one can't budge. Then I try to shift another thing in my life. I'm always worried that if I put another stress on top of the pile, that it is going to be what tips it over the edge and makes it all come crashing down.*

Stress is a physical and psychological reaction to demands placed upon us that we feel are greater than we can handle, like being assigned a twenty-page paper due in a week or having to pay a huge phone bill when you don't have any money. Stress, in little bits, isn't such a bad thing. Without a little bit of stress in life things could get pretty tedious and boring—a little bit of tension in one's love life provides a bit of interesting soap opera drama. If students didn't get a little worked up over their grades, nothing would ever get done. It's stress that motivates you to finally put down the GameBoy and iPod and start making headway on a term paper.

However, there are some major downsides to stress. Too much stress or a buildup of it over time can take a significant toll on a person's physical and mental health. Without a release for it, pressure can build. A tire with too much air in it can burst or spring a leak. The pressure buildup from stress might be expressed in uncontrolled ways like becoming sick or being more irritable than usual. Sometimes, unhealthy ways of managing stress are tried through drinking, drugs, or even eating issues. Finding healthy ways to cope with stress is central to succeeding in college.

Stress Check: Are You …

- Having difficulty sleeping—either sleeping too much or not enough?
- Seeing changes in eating habits—eating more or less than normal?
- Forgetful or feel your mind is racing?
- Irritable, short tempered, or frustrated?
- Suffering from recurring colds and minor illnesses?
- Feeling overwhelmed or disorganized?
- Thinking things like "I can't do it" or feeling under pressure?

Is This a Phase?

> *Most of my friends claim that their freshman year was the toughest. For me, it was smooth sailing until I hit my junior year. I signed up for independent study and was working a part-time job. It was too much. Then, my advisor called me in to tell me that if I didn't finish, I wouldn't graduate. It was like all of a sudden I woke up one day and realized I had less than a year to figure out what I was going to do with the rest of my life. For three years, I had lived in a comfortable little place I like to call denial.*

Each year of college offers a unique transitional hurdle. Feeling a little uncomfortable as you jump over these hurdles is actually quite natural. With each passing year, the hurdles get higher and higher. As the bar is raised, it might be difficult or impossible to jump as high and as fast as you did in the past.

Feeling blue or stressed could be just a normal reaction to a natural phase most people go through as they are faced with new challenges. However, if a student really gets into a rut that he or she can't get out of and friends have moved on, it may be a good idea to make sure feeling blue it isn't more than a normal reaction to an ordinary hurdle. It could be depression, so it's important to be mindful of where stress is coming from!

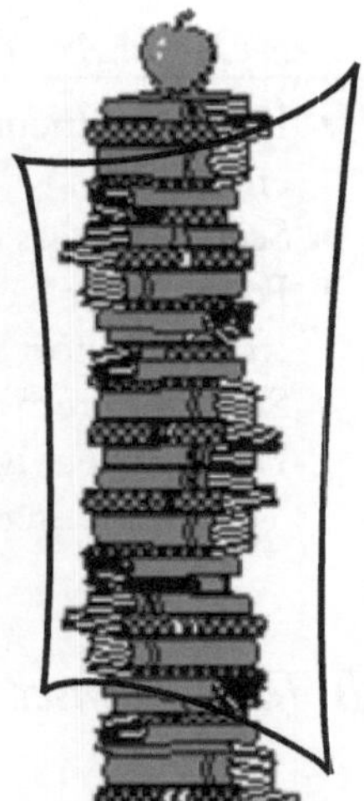

Freshman Year

Freshman year is the quintessential example of the perfect blend of good and bad stress. It's exciting and nerve-racking at the same time. The freedom is too good to be true yet words cannot describe how stressful it is to meet new people, live in a dorm with a virtual stranger, navigate your way through the maze of new classes and activities, and keep up with rigorous new academic challenges, all the while trying to keep one's sanity and cool intact.

Sophomore Slump

The freshman year was so novel and exciting, and this year is "blah" in comparison. As a result, sophomores often become dissatisfied with their lifestyle and relationships. A little bit of anxiety arises as they start to think about the future and career goals. This is the year when many sophomores feel pressured to define their identity.

Junior Jitters

Those who didn't experience the sophomore slump, are bound to find that it kicks in by their junior year. Time is slipping away fast: If you haven't found a major, it's pretty much now or never. This is the year when many juniors start to get anxious about what the future holds. The tough questions that were kept at bay for a while need to be on the front burner this year.

Senioritis

When the grad school papers are snugly in the mail and the postgraduation future is secure, papers suddenly slide by unnoticed, and class attendance goes down. Students inflicted with senioritis relax almost to a comatose state. There may be some regret when seniors look back over their college career, fear of the future, exhaustion from working so hard, and anxiety about the possibility of relationships ending.

Fifth and Sixth Year Seniors

Finishing college in four years is difficult for many students. Stress for fifth and sixth year students may come out of wanting to graduate but not being quite ready. Also, many of their friends have already moved on with their lives. Stress may come from feeling left behind, lonely, or pressured to hurry.

Graduate School

Research labs, teaching classes, a book length thesis, publication, surviving demanding advisors, relationship stress, and internships that verge on slave labor are just a brief snapshot of a graduate student's life stress.

Semester Stress

Check the calendar. It just might be a "normal" time of year to be totally and utterly stressed out. There is often a regular ebb and flow of anxiety and certain kinds of stress that reliably hit during each semester or quarter. September may bring homesickness or difficulty transitioning back into the college environment. Around December, holiday break stress arrives. Valentine's Day can bring up worries about one's relationships or lack of relationships. Then, concern about where to spend spring break hits. May often brings worries about what to do for the summer. At this point, some students are uncomfortable about returning home or leaving the school environment. So, don't forget to consider whether you are experiencing "normal" stress.

Desserts Spelled Backward Is Stressed: Stress and Health

So, what if you can't seem to relax? This might actually be damaging your overall health. Not surprisingly, studies have found a significant correlation between unhealthy eating and stress (Anding et al. 2001; Hudd et al. 2000; Kitsantas, Gilligan, and Kamata 2003). Students who report high levels of stress indicate that they eat less fruit and vegetables than nonstressed students and feel they are in poorer health (Hudd 2000). In contrast, students who report low amounts of stress describe themselves as being in fairly good health. Nonstressed students not only eat more fruits and vegetables but get more exercise. It makes a pretty good case for finding healthy ways to manage stress.

Emotional Eating: What's Eating You?

When we are stressed out, we eat. When we are bored, we eat. When we are angry, sad, lonely, or tired or any other emotion, we eat. We use food as a way to anesthetize pain, cover up feelings, or fill up an emotional void. When we are using food in these ways, we are doing what is called "emotional eating." The food creates a smoke screen in front of the feelings. This is why it is so important to be in touch with your emotions. Identifying the feelings helps you to understand what's behind your eating: is it to satiate hunger or is it to get a grip on emotions? If the feeling is identified as, say, boredom, there are other ways to deal with this feeling—maybe by flipping on the TV or reading a book.

Being mindful of your feelings enables you to get a good handle on certain emotions that repeatedly trigger eating. Many of us have to work really hard to identify what feelings exactly have this effect. Sometimes it is obvious, but other times it is not. It's likely that the feeling–food connection happens with such regularity that it takes place subconsciously or below our awareness. For example, a student might find herself snacking at the refrigerator but not know why. The feeling that prompted her to eat wasn't obvious or she was not conscious of it.

Maybe she is emotionally eating now because she is still upset about a fight she had with her boyfriend two days ago. It's hard to make the link between the two events—the eating and being upset.

Eating Your Heart Out

Disordered Eating and the Quagmire of Emotions

Everybody eats for emotional reasons now and then. But, for people with eating problems, there is a much deeper and chronic connection between eating and regulating their feelings. Eating, not eating, purging, or restricting food is the primary way people with food problems deal with their emotions.

The type of eating issue a person has often defines the unique challenges he or she will likely have around food and feelings. For example, people who restrict their food are generally uncomfortable with strong feelings. Cutting off from food is a way to break away or strip away the emotions that feel unmanageable or uncomfortable. People who restrict food tend to be so shut off from their feelings that they have trouble even knowing what their feelings are, and are unable to articulate them out loud. In contrast, people with mindless overeating and chaotic mindless eating have lots of emotions. They are brimming with intense, turbulent emotions going on inside that sometimes feel out of control. Someone with chaotic mindless eating tendencies may feel the need to get rid of the feelings, which parallels their experience with food. They purge their body of food and emotion. Finally, chronic mindless overeaters just can't seem to feel enough or get to the emotion they desire. They continue to eat and eat as a way to try to fill up an emotional emptiness. But no matter how much they eat, food just never seems to fill up that hole in their heart.

A big part of overcoming eating issues is helping people to be more mindful of their feelings. It's important to realize that feelings can be scary but you don't have to be afraid of them. People with eating issues get stuck. They know the food "works" to fix their feelings, at least temporarily, and have a hard time seeing other healthy options for coping with their feelings. Therapy can help people unravel the psychological connection between food and emotion.

Gut Feelings

The connection between food and feelings is so strong, it even comes across in our everyday language and vernacular. For example, there are many food words that are used to describe feelings. Delete emotion and insert food word.

He's such a ham!
She's the salt of the earth.
You're a peach.
You are a nut.
Don't stew about it.
Apple of your mother's eye.
Red as a beet.

I'm So Stressed Out: Mindfully Coping With Stress

Nothing is going to make stress magically disappear. A three-day relaxation retreat in a luxury spa (although probably well deserved and warranted in the situation) is not in the cards.

Stress Management Methods (Without Food)

The following are simple, one-minute stress management techniques. They are based on mindfulness skills. Even if these tips reduce stress levels by one notch from an eight to a seven (on a scale of ten), it's worth giving them a try.

Aware: Breathe: Really breathe. Inhale. This is perhaps the easiest and quickest way to reduce stress. Breathing exercises are painless and take only a few moments—in the dorm, in class, or during a lecture. This is a special kind of breathing. It's about focusing all of your attention on how you breathe. Pay attention as the air travels through the nostrils. Count in and out while exhaling. Imagine that there's a balloon in your stomach. As you breathe in, the balloon is expanding. Focus on that image. How does breathing help? During sleep or when totally relaxed, we tend to breathe very slowly. So, if breathing is consciously slowed down, the body can be tricked into believing that it is moving into a state of rest. When breathing slows, the body sends signals to the brain to shift into relaxation mode. The body can't be relaxed and stressed at the same time.

Observe: "Don't feel that way." "You shouldn't be sad." Sound familiar? Our friends and loved ones often encourage us not to feel the way we do. We even tell ourselves to quit feeling sad or disappointed. The truth of the matter is that you feel what you feel. If everyone wasn't in such a rush to push feelings away, perhaps people wouldn't turn to things like food, to try and make it better.

Instead of trying to quiet emotions or rid yourself of them, feelings should be accepted, and then they can be managed to the best of your ability. This makes so much more sense. When a feeling exists, simple notice it, watch it. Every feeling doesn't have to be responded to. You don't, for example, have to act on anger by yelling or throwing things.

Being in the moment: A key aspect of being mindful is to slow down and taking it *one step at a time.* Although it may seem paradoxical, slowing down will help improve academic performance. Multitasking divides up attention and makes you less aware of what you are doing. It leaves room for mistakes, which can stress you out even more. We waste an enormous amount of time and energy cleaning things up that we really didn't think through. The best advice is *pace, not race*. Live one, prioritized moment at a time.

Nonjudgment: *Don't fight it!* If a problem exists, it is helpful to consider whether the struggle is against actually having a problem; for example, "I don't want to deal with this" or "I don't want to have this problem." Too much time is spent being angry and wallowing. Nonjudgmentally accepting the issue is the first step to being able to move on to finding a good solution. Instead say, "I don't like it, but I can work through it."

Acceptance: If you can't get rid of stress, you need to learn how to cope with it. Try some quick and easy relaxation exercises.

1. **Be a limp rag doll:** Close your eyes. Imagine that you are a rag doll. Let go of your shoulders. Allow your head to gently fall to one side and then gently to the other side.
2. **Say ommmmmm:** Strike a few yoga poses (see www.yogajournal.com). Yoga has been clinically proven to increase relaxation, increase muscular strength, and reduce weight. Exercise doesn't have to be excruciating and high exertion to reap some mood enhancing benefits. Going to a short yoga class has been shown to help improve mood and stress level (Netz and Lidor 2003).
3. **Tension tamer:** Try shoulder shrugs. Lots of people carry their anxiety in their shoulders or even in their neck. They sometimes don't even realize they are tensing these muscles. Expressing tension in this way can lead to stiff muscles, pain, and headaches. Slowly raise one shoulder. Then, drop it. Raise the other shoulder and then drop it. Make sure to do these shoulder lifts slowly. Keep your neck and spine straight and face straight ahead. Then, try raising them together. Hold for a moment, then drop them down. Repeat.
4. **Five-minute chill out:** For just five minutes, let go of whatever is on your mind and just be present. Give yourself a minivacation from your worries. Let your mind drift as if on a raft floating down a quiet river or hiking in the Rocky Mountains. Sit or lie down. Put down the books and turn off the TV. Put your feet up. Set your alarm for ten minutes to prevent falling asleep or worrying about the time. Clear your head of clutter. Try to find tranquil thoughts by just listening to the noise around you.

Chapter 8, Mindful Eating 101: Improving eating habits may actually have less to do with what is eaten and more to do with how emotions are managed. Getting a handle on stress and feelings may be one of the most important steps taken on the path to eating more mindfully. Watch your feelings, don't push them away. Find healthy ways to manage stress and emotions that don't involve food or eating.

Part Two

Mindful Eating

Chapter 9

Using the F-Word (Fat)

Twelve "Body Language" Statements That Encourage Mindless Eating and the Fear of Fat

"You're Fat"

I took my new boyfriend shopping to help me buy a pair of jeans for a "lumberjack party." Flannel shirts and jeans were a must to enter. The highlight of the party was wading through freshly cut woodchips and keg races.

After I put on the first pair, I shyly came out of the dressing room and did the obligatory slow twirl so he could get the 360-degree perspective. I noticed myself circling a little more quickly when my butt was center stage until I was safely facing him again. I asked, "How do I look? He was silent for a moment, crossed his arms and looked at me thoughtfully. His eyes scanned up and down my body. The scrutiny was enough to make even a supermodel just the tiniest bit uncomfortable. Then, he said, "Those jeans make you look fat."

My mouth dropped open. Did he just call me fat? Had I had my hearing checked lately? In an instant, the relationship was over. I was already envisioning the look of outrage on my friends' faces when I recounted this story. I imagined sitting in my dorm room with my two roommates. They would hand me a tissue and reassure me that I wasn't fat. I already knew I wasn't extremely overweight but I had amnesia at the moment. This would be a legendary story about him and no girl, I hoped, would ever want to date him again. At parties, when he walked by women would nudge each other, raise an eyebrow, tilt their head toward him and whisper, "He's the guy who calls women fat."

I was brought back to reality when the curtains of the next dressing room fluttered and a head poked out just long enough to get a look at the two of us. The girl in the next dressing room had overheard the entire transaction and I imagine she just wanted to sneak a peak at what a boyfriend 101 flunkie actually looked like.

The rage was building and I composed myself enough to open my mouth to respond. He saw my lips quivering and the anger flashing in my eyes. I know that I'm not crazy about my thighs but I'm fairly happy with my body and there was just no need for an insult of that kind. He could have just said, "Let's keep looking for another pair."

Luckily, he responded just in time before I had the opportunity to speak. He got a devilish grin on his face and said "Yep, you look phat. He spelled it out slowly—p-h-a-t, which of coarse is the slang word for hot. He tacked onto the end, "I think you'd look great in anything." Suddenly, it clicked. He was just kidding and trying to get a reaction out of me. I forgot that phat had multiple meanings. Depending on how you said it and technically how it was spelled, it was a compliment. I didn't realize how sensitive I was to a single three-letter word. Upon hearing it and being labeled with it, I was ready to abandon my relationship without any questions asked.

Sticks and Stones

Who ever came up with the sticks and stones theory must have been in some serious denial because words do hurt. They hurt a lot. No words are more powerful or damaging than the destructive words we use to describe our bodies: *fat, chunky, chubby, tubby, slob.* You might cringe a little at these words. You are likely to react quite differently to words like *vivacious, gorgeous, head turner, stunning.*

Many of us are experts at belittling ourselves. We know just how to manipulate harsh terms to really make them hurt. The words we use are like steel wool pads on our self-esteem. My clients are brutally honest about the harmful vocabulary words they mercilessly attach to their bodies. *Bessie the cow, fatso, pig* are just a few of the words I am able to repeat out loud. Harsh words like these sit right on the tip of the tongue ready to be unleashed at a moment's notice.

Unfortunately, dagger sharp words come out with surprising ease. They escape our lips automatically and effortlessly. One client likened her mirror to a motion detector that flips on a light. When she passed her reflection in a mirror, it triggered a switch in her brain. Instantly, the insults came streaming out of her mouth. It happened quickly and without a second thought. She hardly had a moment to say to her mind, *stop*!

Mindless Speech

While we are free with insults and generous with critical words, many of us don't really stop to ask ourselves whether there's harm in this kind of talk. Am I just flapping my gums or do I really take to heart what I say? In some ways, it is like the nonchalant question, "How are you?" We ask store clerks and acquaintances this question frequently. It's a pleasantry we ask mindlessly. We don't even really expect a response beyond "Fine, thank you." When someone breaks the typical routine and recounts a detailed description of their awful day, it's a genuine surprise. It's a stark reminder that we use common phrases all the time without really thinking about what we are doing.

People talk about their bodies with the same kind of detached awareness. "I'm so fat!" It's a statement we often repeat and we really don't stop and closely examine what we are saying. Yet, this word can rock us to the core. Judgmental descriptors cut at us like scissors and rip to shreds even the strongest self-esteem.

As if it wasn't enough to beat ourselves up, we turn our vengeful tongues on others. We say equally critical and cruel words to pummel the self-esteem and confidence of friends, partners, and family members. Here is a story told by one of my clients about the destructive nature of words.

> *In my business economics class, we were instructed to form small focus groups. Our task was to make a company work more efficiently and get rid of excess waste. After the first half hour of working together in class, our group realized that we had way too many people to be productive. The professor chose Anna, one of the smartest business majors in our class. I'm sure he delegated her to the other group because she would make valuable contributions. As all eyes focused on her, I suddenly felt embarrassed for her. She had difficulty getting out of the chair due to her large, overweight frame, and her awkwardness was compounded by the stares of her classmates. As she walked a few feet, one of the boys whispered under his breath, "Well, I guess we can say we are officially trimming the fat from our group." Now, when I overeat, I hear those words in my head. They weren't even about me but those kind of hateful words just can't slide off of me.*

Mindful Speech

Mindful speech is the polar opposite of critical language. It is factual, gentle, kind hearted, and free from harm to yourself or others. When you get right down to it, much of the words people use are not factual. If you tell yourself that you are "dumb," it might just be a feeling not a fact. Self-descriptions are frequently filtered through a screen of self-doubt and a very distorted body image.

Mindful words, in contrast, are compassionate and nonjudgmental. They are adjectives cloaked in self-acceptance and don't contain harmful language that relates to teasing, judgment, and criticism. The power of language is recognized and revered. Mindful speech is done with a watchful eye. The speaker's words are carefully chosen. They do not just repeat empty, mindless phrases. When choosing what to say, the statements are thoughtfully considered. The speaker watches intently to see how their words affect the other person. The speaker notices whether his or her comment produces a smile or a crestfallen face that falls silent. Sometimes words slip out before we can do anything to stop it. Or, they have an effect that we wouldn't have predicted. When it happens, you say compassionately, "I'm sorry, I didn't mean for my words to upset you but it looks like what I said hurt you."

Why Is Mindful Speech Important?

Language guides your actions. The positive or negative connotations of your vocabulary affects mood and behavior. For example, is a dandelion a weed or a flower? If it's a flower, it's put in a vase, and gazed upon. It might even be given as an affectionate present. But, if it's described as a weed, it's likely to be mowed down without a second thought or tossed to the side when planting a garden. It's easy to tread a weed underfoot.

One of my clients frequently referred to her body as "disgusting garbage." Needless to say this translated into the way she treated herself. When she deleted the negatives and inserted more sensitive, kind words about her body, she began using adjectives such as *valuable* and *precious*. Imagine the difference.

Twelve Mindless Eating Statements

"I'm a piece of rubber. You're a piece of glue. Whatever you say bounces off of me and sticks to you." Wouldn't it be nice if it were that easy? It's likely though that we need more than a little jingle to help us know what to do with hurtful words.

Here is where mindfulness enters. Simply be more aware of the kind of language you use to describe yourself. Negative thoughts happen effortlessly and below your awareness radar screen. Below is a list of a few common phrases. As you read this list, ask yourself whether you say these critical statements. If so, that's okay. Remember not to "judge" yourself for doing it. Just be more mindful of toxic language.

1. **I feel fat:** "I wear a size eight jeans. My friends say I look really thin but when I look in the mirror, I think to myself I should be skinner. I say out loud, 'Ugh, I feel so fat.' I can't understand why one of my friends, who is smaller than I am, also feels fat. Does everyone feel fat no matter what size she is?"

Whether you are a size two or a twenty-two, the majority of us would admit that they have felt fat at one time or another. But, unless you are on the upper tier of the BMI chart, feeling fat, often has very little to do with your actual weight. Instead, feeling fat is really about feeling *bad* about something (Anderson 2000; Eldredge, Wilson, and Whaley, 1990, Striegel-Moore, McAvay, and Rodin, 1986). The fat feeling pops up when we think we are not good enough or don't measure up to some kind of standard. In this sense, fat is used in lieu of a feeling or an adjective.

Why are we so stuck on this word? Almost everyone understands what it's like to feel fat. It's a shorthand term used to sum up how you feel in one simple little three-letter word. Sure, sometimes, feeling overweight may actually be about wishing you were thinner. Yet, at other times a negative emotion leads people to feel fat.

Mindful speech tip: When you say "I feel fat," remember to carefully consider *why* you feel that way. Is it prompted by a physical sensation like overeating? If so, a more accurate description is "I feel full." Or, in the case of the tight pair of jeans that pinch at the waist, it would be more to the point to instead say, "These jeans are really uncomfortable."

It's particularly important to notice when the word *fat* is used as a substitute for an emotion (Anderson 2000). Remember that "fat" is not a feeling and should not be used as an emotion or adjective. It's like saying "I feel blonde or tall." Fill in the blank with other feeling words/adjectives besides fat. For example, I feel angry at myself, annoyed, bored, unattractive, and so on. Try it. See what happens. It's often the case that we have to work harder to describe what is really bothering us.

2. **I'm so fat:** "I'm so fat, I wish I had your thighs. Mine are like two huge sausages." The woman uttering these critical words, believe it or not, is standing in the middle of a group of her five closest friends. After she makes a few more disparaging remark about her legs, the other people follow suit and criticize their own bodies.

No movie more vividly depicts the warped social function of degrading our bodies than a scene from the movie *Mean Girls*. In the movie, three attractive high school girls eat their lunch in a school cafeteria. One of the three girls, a very thin, stunningly attractive blonde begins complaining about how fat she is and that she desperately needs to go on a diet. She hopes to lose a few pounds prior to an upcoming dance.

After she finishes critically picking apart her body and weight, she waits expectantly. It's an awkward pause. To her surprise, the girl's friends are silent. No one reassures her nor do they refute her claim of fatness. She sends her friends a look as if to say, "Hey, this is your cue. Here's the part where you chime in." The women appear to wake out of their own thoughts and sudden realize they have neglected an important, obligatory friend "duty." They chime in a rote, stereotypical answer something to the effect of "No you're not, you're so skinny." The effort is halfhearted at best and frankly, we don't buy it. The camera pans back to the star. With the "correct response," the friendship and her self-esteem appear to be momentarily restored and they go on with their gossip and routine as usual. "Fat talk" isn't just about feeling fat. Unfortunately, it's a way people communicate how they feel about themselves and it's a social "cue."

Mindful speech tip: When "fat talk" kicks up, take charge. Change the subject. Pick another topic. Or, point out how dieting and fat always seem to come up in conversation. Don't make it "okay" for normal chitchat to include people tearing themselves down as if they were talking about the weather.

3. **Do I look fat?:** "Do I look fat?" In response to this question, one woman's boyfriend replied, "Well, I wouldn't call you fat, but you're not exactly thin." The answer was not quite what she was seeking. For a few days, she sulked and cried over his answer. She began pestering him again with this question.

Asking "does this make me look fat" can really be a relationship "no-no." It's a no win situation for everyone. No matter how the person answers they can't say the right thing. Friends and parents may be tempted to say, "No, you look incredible. I wish I was that thin!" Yet, if they are cautious and wise, they know this is pretty pointless. When someone asks whether they look fat they obviously don't believe they are thin. If they're reassured that they are "just fine," they are likely to question whether they are just being humored or whether they're being blatantly lied to.

Mindful speech tip: The point is to avoid weight and body related comments at all costs. Often, stating, "You are *not* fat." seems to fall on deaf ears. Instead of, "Does this make me look fat," how about, "Is this a flattering outfit?" Or, even better, hold up two choices and ask which one the person likes better. If you want reassurance that you look nice or someone finds you attractive, it's better to talk about it in a way that isn't related to weight. Or, if you are asked, "does this make me look fat" say, "what makes you ask that question?"

4. **Wow! She's got a nice body:** When you catch a glimpse of ribbed abs, the S curve of a waist, or the small hollow of a back, our first response is often an approving, "nice body." Most of us can't help doing a double take. Heterosexual men and women even admit to checking out the bodies of people of the same sex in a nonsexual way (Torte and Cornelissen 2001).

Celebrities, in particular, get a lot of validation for their arms, legs, and stomachs. Each year, TV shows and magazines vote on the Sexiest Man Alive and award This Year's Best Bodies. They even dismember the person and give glory to a particular body part. Unfortunately, these contests promote the shell-like quality of bodies.

Mindful speech tip: It's okay to appreciate someone's external beauty. We are in constant awe of other natural beauties in the world: the Grand Canyon, a baby's smile, a colorful sunrise. Rather than validating one's body, another way is to say that they have a nice "figure." *Figure* is the word used to describe one's shape. A great figure comes in many different shapes and sizes. A very skinny person often doesn't have a figure. A study of college men and women found that both genders rate a curvaceous body (one with a low waist to hip ratio) as more appealing than one with a low body mass index (BMI) (Torte and Cornelissen 2001). What makes a beautiful person is being fit and having a well proportioned, healthy shape. For women, it's an hourglass figure, muscle tone, definition, curvy hips, and ample breasts that make one have an actual shape. Jennifer Lopez is an actress and musician. She is a great example of a woman whose shape gets more attention than her body. Like Marilyn Monroe, she is noted for her curvaceous body, particularly the shape of her backside.

5. You look so thin: When I think about the many compliments doled out to thin people, I can't help but be reminded of Jessie, an attractive junior who appeared, from the outside, to be the picture of good health. She ran daily, played a varsity sport, and was an excellent student. She talked a lot in therapy about the double edged sword of "thin" compliments. Most of us yearn for compliments about our bodies, but the comments angered her. People had no idea what lengths she went to, and the pain involved in staying thin. In fact, she went about it in very unhealthy ways like excessive exercising. No one knew what she did and how unhealthy it was for her. Unknowingly, people were encouraging and reinforcing her unhealthy, dangerous behavior.

Mindful speech tip: Many eating disorder professionals urge people to strictly avoid commenting on people's weight. This includes positive compliments, praise, and envious statements. Unless you know someone really well, you just don't know how weight related comments will be taken.

6. You can never be too thin or too rich: Mrs. Simpson, wife of King Edward VIII, is often credited with coining the phrase "You can never be too rich or too thin." We definitely know Mrs. Simpson was wrong about the last part. You can be too thin. According to the American Psychiatric Association, a BMI under 18.5 is a serious medical concern and is considered dangerously thin. It's the point at which a person will begin to cause significant physical damage to their body. Many celebrities actually have such low BMIs that they fit into this category.

Mrs. Simpson's quote equates thinness and being rich with being happy. Thinness and happiness are not synonymous. My clients with eating issues have been proof enough of that. One can be very thin and miserable just as easily as one can be over one's ideal body weight and be happy. One reason very thin people can be unhappy is because their bodies are starving. It is very difficult to feel good emotionally when your body is physically breaking down. In fact, a study of college women with eating disorders found that they report a lower level of life satisfaction and higher levels of negative emotion than students who were at risk for an eating issue or those of normal weight (Kitsantas, Gilligan, and Kamata 2003). Happiness is a state of mind, not a number.

Mindful speech tip: Avoid using this phrase and other statements that elevate the value of thinness. Work on substituting statements that value health, like these: "I feel really great after working out," or, "I don't diet, I eat mindfully."

7. **I'm going to start my diet on Monday!**: "I'm on a low carb diet, how about you? I used to be on a low fat plan but that didn't work. I didn't lose any weight. My neighbor tried this diet and she lost a few pounds." Imagine that the woman uttering these words is sitting next to you in a waiting room. As she strikes up this conversation, you immediately notice that she is much thinner than you, fifteen pounds at least. Yet, she chats incessantly about her newest diet. You wonder why she doesn't see that she is thinner than you?

Dieting chitchat should not be taken lightly. While it may feel like just idle conversation or sharing, it isn't. Women who overhear dieting talk report feeling pressure to be thin and are unhappier with their bodies and weight (Stice, Maxfield, and Wells 2003).

Mindful speech tip: Diet chitchat is a part of everyday conversation. But, just because it is common doesn't mean it is helpful nor does it inspire mindful eating. Recognize that talking about dieting can significantly raise people's anxiety. In addition, you might be role modeling unhealthy behavior. Instead, share your endeavors to eat more mindfully.

8. You must have another piece of cake: Ever feel strong armed into eating something when you weren't truly hungry? Maybe you took a second piece of apple pie or another helping of mashed potatoes just to be "polite." Mindless eaters often feel vulnerability to "food pushers." These are people who apply social pressure to eating. For example, your hall mate begs you to eat dinner with her because she doesn't want to go alone. You have a hard time saying no even if you already ate. Or, perhaps your grandmother tells you that she will be "disappointed" if you don't have one of her homemade cookies. It's challenging for mindless eaters to endure feeling impolite turning down food.

People with significant eating problems sometimes need a little coaching with their eating habits. It's important to tell friends and family specifically what they can say to help one maintain a healthy, mindful way of eating. People with eating issues often experience friends, families, and partners as the "Food Mafia," or feel pushed and threatened to eat. The tone can be shaming and critical rather than compassionate and encouraging.

Mindful speech tip: Practice tactful ways to regain control over your food including: "No, thank you"; " I'm stuffed"; "Really, you go ahead"; "I want to wait a few minutes"; "I'm fine, thanks, I'm not hungry, but I'll sit with you while you eat so we can talk."

9. I feel guilty, I shouldn't eat this: "I ate a huge piece of lemon pound cake and two chocolate chunk brownies at a holiday party. They were so good. I savored every bite. But, I broke my diet again. I feel so guilty! I really shouldn't eat sweets."

In the general sense, guilt comes from doing something "wrong" like telling a whopper lie or stealing a roommate's favorite shirt. Yet, with what we eat, there is a lot of latitude in what we can see as "wrong."

The eating "crime" doesn't really relate to the actual "badness" of the behavior but simply how you look at it. For example, you could eat a candy bar on one day and feel fine with this action. The next day you can be racked with excruciating guilt for eating the very same candy bar. The only thing that changed was how you looked at the situation and your negative *evaluation* or *interpretation* of the behavior (Burney and Irwin 2000).

For dieters, guilt and shame can come out of the mere act of eating. The dieter has put so many limitations on food that it has completely warped the way he or she feels about eating. Almost all eating is evaluated by the mind as bad. Guilt can creep up from breaking a food "rule" or "cheating" on one's diet. Or, for overeaters or bingers it comes from feeling they have lost control.

Mindful speech tip: Remember, guilt is all about one's *interpretation* of the event. So, one way to stop creating guilt trips is to change the way you think about food. A good start is to take food out of "good" and "bad" categories. If you point to a cookie and say, "that's bad, I can't eat that and then eat it anyway, you're likely to feel guilt because you've labeled this food as "bad." Saying that foods are good or bad makes eating or not eating a crime or transgression. Instead, focus on food being unhealthy or healthy. Remember that you need to keep telling yourself that it is "okay" to mindfully eat!

Another way to avoid the "I shouldn't eat that" trap is to focus more on the *consequence* to the *action* rather than one's worth as a person. For example, rather than saying, "I'm such a bad person for mindlessly overeating," say, "My stomach really doesn't feel good when I overeat."

Guilt can also come from feeling that you don't deserve to eat. When this happens, it is an important red flag to get some professional help. Remind yourself that eating is a pretty natural and important phenomenon. It gives you the energy to live your life in the fullest sense. Eating in itself, obviously, isn't a bad thing. If you experience a lot of guilty or can't let go of feeling as though you have done something wrong when you eat, some professional help might be needed to understand why you think this way.

10. I need chocolate: "I've had a horrible day. I failed my midterm and lost my twelve-page paper in my computer. I need chocolate, quick!"

Statements that emphasize the need for food in times of crisis and turmoil unfortunately reinforce the misperception that food is the perfect emotional anesthetic. These words suggest that food really possesses the power to temporarily numb out pain and stress. We all have unique tastes when it comes to the foods that give us pleasure. In fact, men prefer warm foods that you'd typically find within a meal such as casseroles, steak, and soup (Wansink, Cheney, and Chan 2003). Women, by contrast, label snack type foods like chips and chocolate as their favorite comfort foods.

Mindful speech tip: When you are craving your favorite comfort food, determine what feeling or event prompted the desire. What kind of comfort are you really in need of? A hug? A break? An encouraging word?

11. What the heck!: Ever throw your hands up in the air and say, "What the heck, I might as well have the cupcake, I already broke my diet for today. What does it matter now? I'm throwing in the towel because there is no way I'm going to eat in a mindful way." This statement is the epitome of a "black or white attitude" or all or nothing thinking. It's either–or with no possible gray area (McFarlane et al. 1999). Thus, this logic boils down to "either I'm very mindful of my relationship to food or I'm absolutely not."

Mindful speech tip: Try to work toward a middle of the road, gray area rather than all or nothing. Go for what's realistic. Maybe I can't pass up the chips but it doesn't mean I have to eat the whole bag.

12. Good job, let's get ice cream: The connection between food and rewards is born early in life. When you skin your knee and you are a "brave boy," you are rewarded with a lollipop. As an adult, a friend might propose a special dinner to celebrate a job promotion.

Food is used to celebrate, reward as well as bribe. "If you do your homework, you can have a cookie." In a study by Strohmetz, Fisher, and Lynn (2002), waitresses even got a bigger tip when they left a piece of candy with the bill versus those who didn't.

The reverse problem is using food to punish. While we love to eat to celebrate life's good moments, there are many people who don't eat as a way to punish or chastise themselves; for example, by sending yourself to bed without dinner. Or, stating that you don't deserve to eat because you were "bad" and mindlessly overate.

Mindful speech tip: Notice when you try to use food as a reward or punishment (Strohmetz, Rind, Fisher, and Lynn 2002). Avoid thinking of a chocolate cake or Ruben sandwich as something "special" rather than just another food. Elevating the status of an edible item runs the risk of making all foods a potential weapon or gift. It implies that food is a luxury versus a necessity to live. Remember, food is just food.

Mindful Eating 101: Speech Contract

I agree to be more *aware* of how I talk about food, my body, and weight.

I agree to try to speak positively about my body rather than criticize or judge my body like a trophy. This means practicing compliments and appreciated my uniqueness.

I agree that saying I "feel fat" and "being fat" are two different concepts.

I agree to not participate in "fat talk" or bond over diet discussions.

I agree not to criticize my own or anyone else's body.

I agree not to compliment people on their weight and instead praise other for their actions.

I agree not to participate in weightism or fatism (making negative judgments about overweight individuals) or thinism (judging people as good, more successful, or happier because they are thin).

I agree to avoid commenting on weight gain or loss.

I accept that there are people who will say hurtful things and mindless negative comments.

I agree to talk about food positively rather than ruminating, obsessing, or discussing the fat or carb content

I agree to introduce healthier topics when people begin to talk about dieting, fat, and losing weight

I agree not to tease other people about their weight or criticize the way they eat.

> ***Chapter 9, Mindful Eating 101:*** You must be just as mindful of what comes out of your mouth as what you put into your mouth. Pay attention to how you chat with yourself and others about food, weight, and eating. To eat more mindfully, have a compassionate, nonjudgmental tongue.

Chapter 10

Mindful Eating

Fifteen Ways to Eat More Mindfully in Dorms and Cafeterias

Mindful Eating Contract

Are you ready to try to eat more mindfully? Make a commitment to yourself to get started!

- I agree to eat mindfully, whether I'm eating a meal, snack, or dessert in the dining hall, a restaurant, or dorm.
- I agree to have a more mindful attitude. I understand that diets don't work and will try to avoid a diet mentality.
- I agree to pay attention to my hunger and energy level.
- I agree to be fully present mentally and physically when I'm eating.
- I agree to talk about mindful eating.
- I agree to take mindful bites. This means opening up my senses with each bite to smell, taste, touch, and feel food. I will experience each bite.
- I agree to make eating a priority rather than an option.
- I agree to stop what I'm doing and give eating my full and undivided attention if I want a snack or a meal.
- I agree to keep healthy food in my dorm room or apartment.

- I agree to be nonjudgmental of other people's eating habits, weight, and body shape.
- I agree that being healthy and living mindfully is my number one goal.
- I agree to "accept" and have compassion for myself and my body as it is.
- I agree to____

Signature:______________________

So, if you have made it to this point in *Mindful Eating 101*, you are probably wondering what is the next step? We know that college food is gross. The salad bar looks unappetizing. Given these facts, how do you eat more mindfully? This chapter has a few practical mindful eating tips to use on a day-to-day basis. Whether you're headed off to the cafeteria, dining in a trendy restaurant, or whipping up some lunch in your own home, here are just a few ways to be more mindful.

This is the part of the book where you start looking for the menus. For some people, this is very frustrating. They just want someone to say "eat this" and it will be fine! Unfortunately, it's not that easy. What is good for *you* to eat is a little like your fingerprint. You have unique tastes and cravings, allergies, and specific nutrient needs. If you are an athlete, for example, you might need more protein and carbohydrates than a student who does little to no exercise. International students are likely to desire certain foods that are unique to their culture but may not be a part of the typical American diet. The trick is to find out what works for you. What's healthy for you might not be right for anyone else. Tailor this information to your particular type of mindless eating. You (and sometimes with the help of a professional), can create your own recipe for success.

Eat, Drink, and Be Mindful

1. **Shift out of autopilot eating:** What did you have for breakfast? Be honest: A bowl of cereal, a soda as you drove to class, a few bites of cold

leftover pizza, or nothing? Many people get stuck in an eating rut. In fact, 76 percent of students in one study reported that they consumed the same foods day after day (Haberman and Luffey 1998).

Notice whether you are stuck in any kind of rut or routine. Variety not only helps you avoid food boredom, it also allows for nutritional balance. Eating bagels day after day may reduce your hunger. However, it won't help you get the right amount of vitamins and minerals. Eat a wide variety of fruits, vegetables, grains, and proteins. Pledge to stop autopilot eating, and develop a more mindful attitude.

2. **Awareness: Dear diary:** One way to increase your eating awareness is to start a food diary. A food journal or log is a technique called "self-monitoring," and it will help you to be more *aware* of what and why you eat. People use self-monitoring in a lot of different ways. It's a tool used by athletes to enhance their sports performance. Self-monitoring also helps people quit smoking and improve their body image (Cash and Hrabosky 2003). First, you establish a baseline and then track changes in performance over time.

It's generally a good idea to keep the diary for a several weeks. From day to day, how much you eat can significantly change. You may even notice decreases or increases in your food intake each month, particularly during holiday seasons. Eventually, you will notice some patterns emerge. Perhaps you eat fast food every Friday night or skip breakfast every Tuesday morning before class.

It's important to have concrete data not just feelings. There is often a significant difference between what you feel is going on and what is actually happening. A bad day can convince you that you've made no progress in changing your mindless eating. But, if it's written down in black and white it's hard to let your feelings sway your opinion. It's a little bit like keeping track of your savings account. If you tried to keep it balanced just by recollecting and estimating how much money you spent, you could really get into trouble. And remember, this diary isn't a work of fiction. No one has to read it, so feel free to be honest and let loose. A food diary is one of the few times you can really focus on yourself. Try writing in a diary or journal. Or, create a free online version (see Homework 1).

Homework 1: Food Diary

	How hungry am I?	Food I ate	Thinking/feeling How I felt before and after I ate
Breakfast:			
Snack:			
Lunch:			
Dinner:			

3. Observe: Coming to your senses: When you eat mindfully, you can still enjoy the foods you crave, like pepperoni pizza, Wendy's hamburgers, and M&Ms. Unfortunately, diet books warn us to never, ever eat the snacks that taste great. But, we can't totally give up the foods we enjoy. It isn't realistic. Rather than avoid them, the trick is to eat them mindfully. So when you are ordering pizza with a group of friends, it doesn't mean you have to say "I pass." Instead, you use all the skills you've learned in this book. For example, assess your hunger level. Maybe you will have half a piece or you will have three slices. It just depends. Remember to slow down. This helps you eat the right portion size (see Homework 2).

Try the chocolate meditation right now. In the future, you can adapt it to use with other kinds of foods.

Homework 2: The Chocolate Meditation

Eat chocolate mindfully. To do this exercise, small bite-size candy bars work well. Try candy with crunch/M&Ms for added texture. Or, use a box of assorted chocolates (you can also use a cherry cordial, raisins, an orange slice, sandwich cookie, etc.). Chocolate can produce a lot of conflicting emotions. We may love and crave chocolate yet many people feel guilty when they eat it. Notice what emotions arise during this exercise. Get into a comfortable position, relax, and close your eyes. Use all of your senses in this exercise.

Pay attention to the process of eating the chocolate. Begin by slowly unwrapping the chocolate from the foil. Observe the shape and color of the chocolate. Silently describe it. Touch it and feel the texture as you pick it up. Bring the chocolate up to your nose, and inhale deeply. Take in a few deep breaths. Follow the scent as it travels to the back of your nostrils. Inhale and exhale deeply for a few moments. Place the chocolate on your tongue. Roll it around on your tongue and against the roof of your mouth. Notice any thoughts that come to mind. Bring to mind words that describe the chocolate: *Smooth, rich, sensual.* Also be aware of any feelings, sensations, or memories that arise. Label any feelings that occur. Some emotions might be positive and others might be negative. Sometimes we feel guilty when we eat chocolate or have a lot of "should or "shouldn'ts" about eating it. Don't try to push these emotions away. Just be present with the feelings and sensations. Focus all of your attention onto the taste and texture. Listen to the sound of your jaw chewing the chocolate. Notice the sensation as the chocolate slides down the back of your throat. Imagine it in your stomach. You've just experienced mindfully eating chocolate from start to finish.

Are you surprised that you can obtain pleasure from a focused concentration on just a little bit of chocolate? This chocolate exercise is a good tool to use when you are most vulnerable to mindlessly eating, when you crave chocolate during the premenstrual part of the cycle, for example. Realistically, you can't do this entire exercise during every single meal. It would take too long. But, you can do an abbreviated version during portions of your meal. *Commit to at least one mindful bite per meal.* Chewing and tasting one spoonful in a mindful fashion will remind you to keep checking in with your body.

4. In-the-moment: When you eat, just eat: Sure, you're busy and have a lot "on your plate." Who has time for a three-course meal? Still, eating should be a priority rather than an option or side task. If you get the urge to snack while doing homework, stop and take a break. Resist the urge to multitask while you eat. Stop studying. Devote 100 percent of your attention to your behavior and food. Try turning off the TV or other distractions like the radio which tend to increase the likelihood of mindless eating (Gore, Foster, Dillo, Kirk, and West 2003).

A study has shown how dividing your attention between two tasks can interfere with mindful eating. Participants listened to a detective story while they ate a meal. Women listening to a detective story while they ate versus those who just focused on their eating ate 15 percent more (72 additional calories) and enjoyed their food less (Bellisle and Dalix 2001). Pay attention to your food.

5. Taking your hunger temperature: "I could eat a horse"; "I'm starving to death"; "I eat like a bird." These statements are referring to extreme levels of hunger. On the contrary, "I'm stuffed," "I'm bursting at the seams" signify feeling overly full. Notice that these phrases are all about extreme levels of fullness and hunger. We often have a really hard time understanding *degrees* of hunger. Each time you take a bite, ask yourself, "How hungry am I on a scale of one to ten?" Don't wait until after you are done with your meal. It's like taking your temperature. You don't want to be too hot or too cold. Aim to eat until you are satisfied, not stuffed or starving. Use this chart to help you identify different levels of satiation.

Homework 3: Mindfulness of Hunger Scale

Taking Your Hunger Temperature

With each bite, check in with your stomach. Really get to know the varying degrees of your hunger and fullness.

10 Starving. I feel weak, low energy and grouchy.
9 Uncomfortably hungry. I am thinking a lot about food and planning what to eat.
8 Very hungry. I want to eat now.
7 Pretty hungry. I could eat a meal.
6 A little bit hungry. I could use a snack.
5 Satisfied. I'm not hungry and not too full.
4 Okay. I feel like I just ate a snack. I could still eat one or two more bites.
3 Comfortably full. I feel like I just ate a solid meal.
2 Very full. I ate more than I should have. My "eyes were bigger than my stomach."
1 Overly stuffed. I am uncomfortable. I feel like I just ate Thanksgiving or a holiday meal.

6. Nonjudgment: On the tip of your thoughts: Notice the *way* you think versus *what* you think. Is your thinking like a Ping-Pong match? One side of your brain tells you "it's okay to eat that burger" and then the other side slams back with "no you can't, you fatso." Like Ping-Pong matches, these thoughts can fly back and forth so fast that they can make you dizzy. Be very aware of the way your thoughts influence your food choices (see Homework 4). Just because you think something doesn't mean you have to act on it or let the thought sway your emotions. A thought is just a thought, not a fact.

Homework 4: The School of Thought

Many of us don't listen to or act on every thought that creeps into our brain, particularly when we don't like what we are thinking. Thoughts hum quietly in the back of the mind until you turn your attention to them and turn up the volume. When you ignore the activity happening in the back of the brain, your subconscious can take control.

When you sit down for a meal, really listen to what is going on inside your head. Be mindful of the way your thoughts, or inner voice, control your fork. In this exercise, you compare your thoughts to familiar people in your life. This is to signify that your inner voice or thoughts have different tones and agendas. When you hear a thought fall into one of these categories, just label it. Say to yourself, "Oh ya, that is my red pen or my inner critic talking again. It's the part of me that is really hard on myself." Labeling thoughts brings them out of hiding from below your awareness. See if any of these internal voices sound familiar.

The Professor: The voice of reason and intellect. It's the facts stored in your brain. For example, you know how many fat grams are in a donut, that osteoporosis is linked to calcium deficiencies, and the number of fruit and vegetable servings recommended by the government food pyramid. It's the thoughts that draw on science and statistics. No feelings, just facts.

The Red Pen: The critical, harsh reviewer. It's the voice repeating over and over again, "I'm so overweight," "I hate looking in the mirror," "I'm so bad for eating that piece of pecan pie." No matter how you word the critical feedback, the underlying message is that you aren't good enough and you should do better.

The Insecure Self: The part of you that worries about what other people think. Could she like me? Will people whisper behind my back if I gain the freshman fifteen? The jealous, competitive, insecure part of you that covets someone else's eating habits or gorgeous body.

The Perfectionist: The internal voice that sets your expectations very high and believes you should be "perfect." At times, these expectations are set so far out of reach that disappointment is inevitable. These thoughts are unrealistic and sometime push too hard.

The Partier: What the heck? You only live once. Why not live it up? Isn't college supposed to be the best time of your life anyway? Have another bowl of chips because they taste really good. Forget the consequences. Act impulsively. Eating is all about pleasure.

The Regret: You hear this voice after eating mindlessly. You feel heavy or sick to your stomach. It's a direct result of eating too much/ignoring fullness. These thoughts typically starting out with "I should have… or I wish I wouldn't have…. Or I knew at the time I should not have…" It's the voice of regret.

Your Conscience: The guilty voice. "Finish your plate. Don't you know there are kids starving in the world." "Are you eating your fruits and vegetables?" This is the inner voice that feels lucky to have food and wants to appreciate being so fortunate.

Your Best Friend: Supportive, understanding, and empathic. It's also the wise part of your brain that draws on your past experiences. It puts the whole situation into perspective. "It's okay, so today was a difficult eating day. You skipped breakfast and ended up overeating at lunch. That happens. Tomorrow is a whole new day and you know what a setup it is to skip breakfast." This inner voice knows you really well.

Your True Love: "I love you for who you are, you don't need to lose any weight." "You are perfect to me and don't need to change." These thoughts spring from a nurturing and loving part of yourself.

The Cheerleader: "You can do it!" "Keep fighting the urge." "You're the best." These positive self-statements and thoughts keep your attitude upbeat.

7. **Gray areas: Read my hips, no new diets:** You might be thinking, okay, I know dieting isn't such a great idea, but what am I supposed to do? What are my alternatives? The overarching societal message is don't diet and don't overeat. There is just as much data on the dangers of overly restricting food intake as there is about the health consequences of obesity. The clear instruction is about what *not* to do. What you "should" do is not quite so obvious. What is the middle of the road or the gray area?

Many therapists recommend "natural," "intuitive," "conscious," and "mindful eating" (McFarlane et al. 1999). These approaches urge people not to diet. Instead, they should use their gut instincts to listen to when they are hungry and full. It's what *Mindful Eating 101* is all about. Many people ask, what is normal or mindful eating? While there is no textbook answer, check out the "normal, mindful eating" checklist (see Homework 5).

Homework 5: The Normal, Mindful Eating Checklist

What Is Normal (aka Mindful) Eating?

After years of dieting, it's hard to know what mindful eating is exactly. Here are some guidelines that may help. Check off the ones that describe you.

- ☐ I use my intuitive mindfulness (how I feel inside) with mindfulness of facts (nutritional knowledge).
- ☐ I eat the equivalent of three meals a day (with the addition of snacks).
- ☐ I don't eat according to strict "food rules."
- ☐ I'm flexible about the time, place, and kinds of foods I eat.
- ☐ I eat junk food and sweets in moderation.
- ☐ I don't "diet" (I don't approach food with the mindset of restriction).
- ☐ I do have healthy limits on how much I eat (putting up the stop sign is guided by feeling full rather than fear of getting fat).
- ☐ There are no absolutes like I must not eat a donut or I can never touch a brownie.
- ☐ I am aware of nutrition and its effect on the body.
- ☐ I try to eat to be healthy rather than to satisfy weight or appearance goals.
- ☐ I continue to eat until I am satisfied.
- ☐ I recognize when I'm eating for emotional reasons.
- ☐ I eat foods I really like.
- ☐ I am able to forgive myself and not freak out when I overeat or eat mindlessly.
- ☐ Food is not the center of my life.

8. Food for thought: It's really important not to skip meals. Maybe you've been tempted to pass over dinner because you don't want to interrupt a productive study session in the library. The problem with missing meals is that getting too hungry is a significant trigger for mindless overeating (Nash 1999). When people are really hungry, they aren't too choosy about what they eat. At the point of extreme hunger, they are more likely to reach for the most convenient food (which is typically fast food or junk food) or they just grab anything!

The other reason not to skip meals dates back to the Stone age. Hunger is a basic survival mechanism. It's the signal that food is needed. The sensation of hunger is encoded into our system to alert us to when food is necessary in order to survive. Just in case you miss your stomach's signals, there is a backup plan. Next, you are hard wired to think about food. If you've tried dieting or restricting, you've experienced this first hand. People who are hungry or restricting their food intake tend to think about eating all the time. It's tough to study when all you can focus on is hot pancakes dripping with butter and warm maple syrup.

9. **Mindfully chewing on the fat:** When you are mindful, you maintain a neutral stance while closely observing an emotion. You watch the feeling come, you watch its intensity, and then you watch it grow fainter until it is gone. Our natural human reaction is to act on the feeling immediately. As soon as it happens, you jump rather than take the sidelines and wait. "Don't just stand there, do something!" your mind screams.

Being mindful is just observing. If you watch the feeling, sometimes it may take only a few minutes for the feeling to fade, and other times it may take hours or even days. This watchful state keeps the usual reaction in check. You don't freak out or panic. You learn that things that seem unbearable become bearable.

Take for example "feeling fat" or "guilty" for overeating. For many of us, feeling fat or guilty for what you eat are two emotions that are totally unbearable. As soon as the thought or feeling arises, you don't know how to manage it and want to get rid of it. The discomfort is overwhelming. You desperately want to respond or take action. Anything to quickly rid yourself of the uncomfortable feeling. This is when solemn vows to start dieting start passing your lips. Or, you come up with self-punishments like saying, "I'm never going to eat again." Maybe we are serious, but more likely the vow to not eat is made to alleviate the guilt. It's reduces your anxiety because you can breathe a sigh of relief and say to yourself, "Ah, I have a plan."

Instead of a self-flogging, just watch that uncomfortable feeling as if watching the waves of a tide rise and fall. Notice the fat feeling or guilt rising within, notice the intensity of it and hang in there until it fades. Because, eventually, as all things do, the feeling will likely fade in intensity. Don't react. Respond mindfully. Watch rather than act on the emotion.

10. A mindful environment: Painter, Wansink, and Hieggelke (2002) at the University of Illinois looked at the interaction between how much people eat and where they store snack foods. The researchers placed jars of chocolate kisses in three places in an office. The subjects ate more chocolate kisses when they were easier to reach and visible. On average, the workers ate 5.7 (placed in desk), 8.6 (on desk), 3.0 (two meters away) pieces of chocolate.

If your dorm room looks like the junk food aisle in the grocery store, just putting the snacks out of sight could cut down significantly on mindless eating. It's a pretty easy step. It's "okay" to have junk food, but for mindless overeaters, it may help to keep it in a cupboard. Painter et al. (2002) suggested that keeping a "fruit bowl" handy is likely to increase the consumption of healthy foods. Put a bowl of granola bars, graham crackers, fruit, or healthy snacks in an easy to spot location.

11. Cry not French fry: Boredom, frustration, procrastination, and stress as well as a myriad of other feelings can trick us into thinking we are physically hungry. Painful feelings give us a great excuse to mindlessly overeat. If this is the case for you, it's important to figure out what emotions "trigger" eating. Once you identify the emotion, try to find other ways to deal with the feeling. For example, if you are bored, call someone, send a text message, or write an e-mail (see Homework 6).

Homework 6: Emotional Band-Aids

To avoid using food to fix your feelings, create a menu of nonfood alternatives. Don't wait until you are holding a candy bar to try to figure out other ways to deal with your feelings. Be prepared.

My Top Five Stress Relievers or Emotional Band-Aids

Remember to be specific. Instead of writing "call a friend," write down the friend's name and a backup in case they aren't home.

My Top Stressors

1.
2.
3.
4.
5.

My Top Five Emotional (nonfood) Band-Aids

1.
2.
3.
4.
5.

12. **Eat, drink, and be merry:** If you should choose to drink alcohol (and are of age), it's important to have some information about the relationship between eating and drinking. First, alcohol has a lot of empty (nonnutritious calories). It is no substitute for food. One beer has approximately the same number of calories as a hotdog. So imagine if you drank three beers it would be roughly equivalent in calories to eating three hot dogs. Yuck! A portion of the weight gain that students experience comes from beer, wine, and hard alcohol (see www.factsontap.org).

Alcohol and other substances may make you lose touch with your true hunger. When your senses are dulled or altered by a substance, you may have a sudden craving. You may even think you are hungrier than you are. So, you might find yourself making a late night trek to Taco Bell or ravenously downing an entire bag of Doritos.

The amount of food you have in your stomach impacts the rate at which alcohol is absorbed into your system. Food affects the rate at which blood alcohol levels rise (i.e., you haven't eaten a solid dinner or are dieting versus consuming a well balanced dinner such as pizza or a cheeseburger with fats and proteins; see www.baczone.biz for an explanation). To trace the path of alcohol in your body, alcohol myths, and the consequences of alcohol use see www.collegedrinkingprevention.gov/students/ for details.

13. Tis' the season to be mindful: People with eating issues often struggle with the holidays for several reasons. Going home could mean an awkward adjustment to life under your parents' roof again. Old rules and curfews suddenly resurface. Even if you missed your family and love seeing them, annoying family habits can be magnified after you have been away from them. If you live at home during the semester, you may just find yourself spending much more time there during the breaks.

Holiday breaks also fall immediately after very academically stressful times. It's your time to recover from exams or midsemester stress. Physically and emotionally, you might not be up to par. Prepare your family for what kind of condition they can expect to see you in when you get home, and how you plan to recoup. Also, mentally prepare for any potential areas of conflict. Think about how you are going to explain the new bellybutton ring. Be ready to discuss why you haven't called home recently.

Finally, the biggest challenge is likely to be around food. Obviously, most holidays are filled with sweets and yummy goodies. If the mere thought of stuffing, sugar cookies, and fruit cake stresses you out, it's time to talk to a professional about how to enjoy the day and not let all the food and eating festivities get to you. Check out www.somethings-fishy.org for some tips on eating during the holidays.

14. Buddy up: Find a healthy friend to help you eat more mindfully. Support is always a plus. Remember, your friend has to be on board with a gentle, compassionate, and accepting approach. Be straight with him or her that you don't want to focus on dieting or get stuck in comparisons. Your partner's sole job is to help you to improve your health. Plan to go for a walk three times a week or meet at the gym. Making a breakfast date is a great way to make sure you get up and go.

Many students credit a friend with changing their life. The friend is often the first person they ever told about their mindless eating issues. An accepting and compassionate response from this person was incredibly important. Coach each other on what you need from the other person. Maybe it is "checking in" once a week. Make sure to spell out what you consider a supportive gesture.

15. Mindful eating support: Friends provide an enormous amount of support, but often it's helpful to obtain assistance or a second opinion from a trained professional. The best case scenario involves talking to a friend who has a fairly healthy body image, a person who can just listen empathically and be nonjudgmental. Sometimes it is difficult for nonprofessionals to separate out their own eating issues from yours. For example a friend may try to reassure you that "you're not fat" by stating, "You are so much skinner than I am." This answer isn't very helpful. A response like this actually invalidates how you feel. See appendix A for tips on finding professional support.

Cheat Sheet: The Steps in Mindful Eating

1. Determine your degree of hunger (on a scale of 1–10). This helps identify the right hunger intervention—a snack, a light meal, or a full dinner.
2. Check in with how you feel (are there any emotions involved in making this decision—cravings, feeling deprived, boredom, stress?).
3. Check in with your state of mind (determine how present you are in the moment. Is your mind very focused on what you are doing or is it worrying about something else you have to do that day? Are you acting out of habit or consciously choosing?).
4. Mindfully decide what to eat (check for all of your options, thinking through the consequences of having tuna versus chili, factor in whether you tend to eat this food in a mindful or mindless way).

5. Mindfully take each bite (use your senses, avoid grazing, break out of autopilot eating).
6. Continue to check in with your mind, body, and thoughts as you are eating. Notice any feelings that pop up regarding pleasure, guilt, cravings). Use nonjudgmental, compassionate words to encourage yourself. Frequently ask yourself *"am I eating mindfully right now?"*
7. Pay attention to your body's "stop signs." Mindfully chose when to say "when." Continue to observe the effect of the food on your body after you've finished.

> ***Chapter 10, Mindful Eating 101:*** Whenever you enter a dining hall or cafeteria, use your mindfulness skills. Choose your meals consciously and thoughtfully. When you eat, be aware, nonjudgmental, and in the moment. A few small, mindful steps can start you off toward a lifetime of healthier eating.

Appendix A

When It's More Than Just Mindless Eating

Books, like this one, are a great start to overcoming troubling mindless eating issues. The next step, and sometimes the most appropriate course of action, is to meet with a professional. It's important to consider meeting with a professional if you are having difficulty changing the mindless eating habits on your own or your issues have been going on for a long time.

A mental health professional can help you translate what you read in a book into something directly applicable to your life and unique issues. It's like taking a college class. You can learn about psychology by simply reading a textbook on your own, but for many people, that isn't enough. They opt to read the book and take a class. The professor or instructor adds illustrations, uses examples, and makes it much more tangible. They also limit the scope of the topic to the most relevant and important issues. Eating issues and body image issues are extremely complex and difficult to understand. Consulting an expert can help you comprehend your issues fully without having to do all the research on your own.

Who Can Help You Eat More Mindfully: What Kind of Professional Should You Consult?

If you suspect you might have eating issues or body image concerns, it is essential that you talk to a mental health professional and/or a physician. You might begin by meeting with a college counselor or a doctor at the school health center. These individuals can help assess how serious the concern is and develop a plan of action. If you do have a serious eating issue, it is essential to meet with a qualified and licensed team of professionals which includes a nutritionist, medical monitoring by a psychiatrist and physician, a licensed counselor for individual/group therapy (counselor, therapist, psychologist, a licensed social worker, and a licensed professional counselor). Each professional examines the issue from a different perspective. A therapist looks at the psychological aspects, the psychiatrist focuses on the physical effects of disordered eating, and assesses whether medication is helpful. The nutritionist helps create a food plan. For more information about the types of treatment see www.edreferral.com.

Mindfully Talking to a Friend About Their Eating Issues

- **Observe:** Make a list of behaviors that concern you. Perhaps you notice a shift in your friend's weight, mood changes, skipping meals, or, in the case of a roommate a lot of food is missing. When you are ready to speak to your friend, have some examples on hand to help explain and support your concerns.
- **Communicate nonjudgmentally:** Gently communicate your observations. Set an appointment to talk privately. Make sure you have enough time and it is in a place that you won't be distracted. You don't want roommates walking in and out while you're talking. Most important, use a concerned, nonjudgmental tone. Remember that a person with an eating issue already may be carrying a lot of shame and embarrassment. Use statements like "I'm concerned," or "I'm worried and want to help because I care about you."
- **Listen:** Sit back and give your friend an opportunity to talk. You're job isn't to fix the problem or give any advice, it's just to be sup-

portive and listen. Sometimes the problem isn't really about food. So, being a supportive friend, and listening, no matter what the issue, does a lot to help them heal.

- **Refer:** One of the best things you can do is gather a list of resources to give to your friend. Let them know how to get in contact with a counselor, physician, nutritionist, or other mental health professional who specializes in eating issues. If they want, you can help them take the first steps toward getting help by scheduling the appointment. Offer to join them at their first appointment if they are afraid or they ask you to. However, follow their lead on moving forward. They may not be ready or do not want you to be a part of it. If you are feeling overwhelmed and don't know how to help, meet with a professional yourself to obtain advice or talk to a trusted adult.
- **Then what?** After you have spoken with your friend, your job is to be patient. Give them some time to think about what you've said. Periodically check in and reiterate your interest in how they are doing. Make sure to ask them how you can best be supportive. Do they need space? Would they prefer to talk about it some more? Let them give you instructions on how much they would like you to be involved. If they deny that there is an eating concern, just state your feelings. Often, people don't want to talk about it or are in denial about the issue. Don't push it. You have planted a seed in their brain that you care. When they are ready, they know they can talk to you about it.

Where Do I Find Counseling?

There are many ways you can get treatment or a referral: This book isn't endorsing any particular referral source but helping you to be more aware of the many wonderful resources available. It is a guide to Web sites and campus services that can provide you with more information.

1. **College counseling centers:** Most institutions make some kind of provisions for student counseling. Look on the school's Web site or the student directory phone book under student services, student health center, or the dean of students. They can point you in the right direction. Check out this direct link to many college counseling centers around the country, www.campusblues.com/college_list.asp. Also see: www.ub-counseling.buffalo.edu/vpc.html (The Unabridged Student Counseling Virtual Pamphlet Collection)
2. **Student health center:** Almost all colleges and universities have a student health center. If you don't know where to start, this is probably the best avenue for getting connected to treatment. See the institution's Web site for more details.
3. **Nutritionists and dietitians:** The nutritionist and dietitian are often housed within the student health center, the counseling center, or dining services. Or, go to the Academy of Eating Disorders www.aedweb.org/public/EDsearch.cfm or www.edreferral.com. Both sites will help you locate a professional who specializes in eating issues.
4. **Off site:** Some colleges don't have college counseling centers. If you would like to see someone outside of the university, such as a psychologist in private practice, say, or to go to a mental health clinic, obtain a referral. In addition to ads in the phone book and Web sites, most university health centers or psychological services would be happy to give you a referral to a list of professionals in the area. Another option is to call the state psychology board for their list of licensed mental health professionals and their specialties. Also try the American Psychological Association www.apaonline.org. Finally, you can also obtain a referral anywhere across the nation by calling the National Eating Disorders Association Information and Referral Helpline at 1-800-931-2237 or from NEDA's Web site under the Treatment Referrals section. www.nationaleatingdisorders.org.
5. **Studying abroad:** If you have a history of an eating concern, and are thinking about going abroad, it is probably a good idea

to talk to your counselor first. When students travel abroad, it's not uncommon for them to experience culture shock. The stress, change of environment, lack of social supports, and unfamiliar food can exacerbate even mild food issues.

6. **College athletes:** This segment of the college population is well known to be at-risk for eating issues (Hoyt and Ross 2003). Male and female athletes in sports that emphasize a slender body or low weight are particularly vulnerable to disordered eating habits. This includes sports like gymnasts, ballet dancers, figure skaters, wrestlers, jockeys, swimmers, and distance runners. Athletes and dancers deal with a number of specialized issues that fill up an entire book of their own. See www.gurze.net for a list of books specific to the needs of athletes.
7. **Universities conducting research on eating disorders:** If you are enrolled in a large university or an academically/research oriented institution, you may have access to free, top notch counseling. It is often associated with the Department of Psychiatry attached to a medical school or hospital. Stanford University, Dartmouth College, University of Minnesota, John Hopkins University, The Rutgers Eating Disorders Clinic, and the University of North Dakota are examples of a few schools that often provide innovative therapy to students who agree to be part of one of their research studies (find more on www.edreferral.com/research.htm). Find out first what the study requires and if you meet the criteria. You can also try www.clinicaltrials.gov.

Eating Disorders Advocacy

National Eating Disorders Screening Day

If the university or college you attend doesn't host a screening day, they should! Each year, many colleges and universities participate in the National Eating Disorder Screening Program (NEDSP). How does this help? Researchers contacted a subset of the four hundred colleges two years after they hosted a screening day. Eighty percent of those screened stated that the event helped to make them more aware of the risks of eating issues and that treatment was available (Becker, Franko, Nussbaum, and Herzog, 2004). Also, almost half of those given a recommendation to follow up on their eating sought treatment. The bottom line is that this screening day helps make more people mindful of eating issues and aware of avenues for help.

Web Sites

If you've picked up this book, you've probably already surfed the Web for information on mindless eating. Web sites are an excellent resource. They give us access to an enormous amount of information instantly and with only a few keystrokes. However, one word of caution. The Web, in the grand scheme of things, is still in its infancy. It really hasn't been all that long ago that computers shrank from the size of a room to one you hold in the palm of your hand. A study examined the accuracy and the quality of Web sites (Murphy, Frost, Webster, and Schmidt 2004). Depending on what browser they used, they obtained pretty varied results. At this point, there is no standard credentialing of Web sites—no review boards. Any regular Joe can put up his or her own Web site with grossly inaccurate and even dangerous information on it. So, as you look at Web sites, keep this in mind. It's wise to be very choosy and cautious about the information you gather from the Web.

Antimindful Web Sites: Pro-Ana and Pro-Mia

Pro-Ana and Pro-Mia Web sites are a recent addition to the Internet. Pro-Ana, (proanorexia), and Pro-Mia (probulimia) define anorexia, bulimia, and other eating problems as "lifestyle choices" rather than clinical illnesses for medical and psychological professionals to treat. Consequently, these "lifestyle choice" Web sites do little but promote unhealthy and unsafe dieting and eating habits.

These sites exemplify the dangerous information that students may find on the Internet when searching for help with eating issues and body image. Pro-Ana and Pro-Mia sites are the opposite of self-help Web sites. They are self-hurt sites that often masquerade as self-help sites. Almost all have a "thinspiration" picture gallery to display photographs "ana" beauty ideals— the emaciated bodies of waiflike models. These Web sites promote a severely disordered body image ideal and provide exceedingly dangerous and potentially lethal information. They are not aimed at helping people obtain a healthy relationship with food. The vast majority of mental health and medical professionals are 100 percent against these Web sites and are gravely concerned about their potential harm.

There is much controversy and debate about how we should respond to these Web sites as a society and culture. Without looking very hard, you can find lots of disturbing and harmful information on the Web, including violent pornography and hate Web sites. Fortunately, many of the Pro-Ana and Pro-Mia sites have been shut down by their host search engines. They are becoming increasingly rare and difficult to find.

If you see one of these Web sites or are part of a chat group/live journal that is a Pro-Ana or Pro-Mia society, talk to a mental health professional about that site. Students often say that these sites are "triggers" for negative emotions that are detrimental to their body image and eating problems. Because the sites are new, mental health professionals are currently conducting studies to better understand their effects. As a result, it is best to avoid all contact with Pro-Ana and Pro-Mia propaganda.

Recommended Web Sites on Eating Issues

www.edreferral.com
www.mirror-mirror.org
www.nationaleatingdisorders.org
www.something-fishy.org
www.eatingmindfully.com
www.mindfuleating101.com

Other Helpful Web Sites

Academy for Eating Disorders (AED)
www.aedweb.org

Anna Westin Foundation
www.annawestinfoundation.org

Anorexia Nervosa and Related Eating Disorders, Inc. (ANRED)
www.anred.com

America on the Move
www.americaonthemove.org

BodyPositive
www.bodypositive.com

The Body Positive
www.thebodypositive.org/index.html

Dads and Daughters (DADS)
www.dadsanddaughters.org

Eating Disorders Coalition for Research, Policy & Action
www.eatingdisorderscoalition.org/

Harvard Eating Disorders Center
www.hedc.org/

Healthy Weight Network
www.healthyweight.net

International Association of Eating Disorders Professionals (IAEDP)
www.iaedp.com

Massachusetts Eating Disorder Association, Inc. (MEDA)
www.medainc.org

Montenido
www.montenido.com

National Association of Anorexia Nervosa and Associated Disorders (ANAD)
www.anad.org

National Association to Advance Fat Acceptance (NAAFA)
www.naafa.org

National Center for Overcoming Overeating (NCOO)
www.overcomingovereating.com

The National Eating Disorders Centre (NEDIC)
www.nedic.ca/reading.html
National Institute of Mental Health (NIMH)
www.nimh.nih.gov/publicat/eatingdisorder.cfm#ed5
The Renfrew Center Foundation.
www.renfrew.org

Books

If you are interested in reading more on the subject of mindful eating, check out a book list created by The Renfrew Center, an excellent eating disorder treatment facility in Pennsylvania. They have a comprehensive list of highly recommended books. Visit www.renfrew.org/resources/index.asp.

Also, visit www.gurze.net. This is an online bookstore that only carries books pertaining to eating issues. Send away for their catalog or view it online.

Appendix B

Eating Mindfully at Work

So, you've made it. You've graduated! Thankfully, you have your diploma safely in your hand. That little piece of paper states that you've survived years of hard work and mental sweat. Even better, you have a job all squared away. Thank goodness!

As you are preparing for your new life ahead, you have probably pondered all the little things about college life you will miss. It's a pretty safe bet that cafeteria food is not one of them. In fact, you probably are breathing a sign of relief. No more cafeteria buffet line, mass produced food, Taco Bell runs at 3:00 A.M., or mindless eating while studying until the wee hours of the night. Finally, your waistline is safe.

Don't get too excited. The road ahead actually will bring on a whole new slew of mindful eating challenges. Mindless eating challenges are likely to follow you right out of the dorm room and straight into a corporate office, internship, or graduate school. No matter where you go or what kind of job you secure, there are mindless eating traps everywhere. Getting a solid education in mindful, healthy eating will benefit you no matter what you do with your college education.

1. **The nine to five challenge:** When you start that nine to five job, most of your waking hours will take place at the office. This means you will eat one to two meals a day at work. If you have an early morning commute or work late it may mean eating breakfast, lunch, and dinner at the office.

   Your options are going back to the brown paper days or eating out. The key is planning ahead. Make sure you have enough food with you so you don't get too hungry, which is a major trigger for mindless eating. Pack an extra snack in case you do have to stay late. It's up to you to eat a balanced, health diet to fuel your work day. It's pretty tough to work and concentrate on an empty stomach.

2. **Job interviews:** As part of the interview process, many employers may include a lunch interview. In part, it is to see how you respond to a social setting. However, there is nothing more difficult than eating mindfully during a high stress interview. When you are nervous, it's difficult to be present with your body. You may find yourself eating to avoid talking or not checking in with your body. It's a good idea to eat a light snack before you go. Don't go to the lunch interview or meeting too hungry.
3. **The corporate account:** Do I want dessert? Sure, why not! When some one else is paying for dinner, the word free may interfere with mindful eating. It's tempting to order that expensive, humongous steak particularly when someone else is footing the bill. To avoid mindless eating, remember to eat exactly what you would eat it you were paying.
4. **Opportunity eating:** For one of my clients, every Wednesday morning was bagel day at the office. She looked forward to it and snagged two or three bagels. Normally, she wouldn't eat more than one bagel. But, it was the perception of it being free that motivated her to take full advantage of it. Also, it seemed to make up for some of the things she didn't like about her job. If food is free, we tend to eat it, whether we are hungry or not. Never underestimate the power of a free bagel to induce mindless eating. To remain mindful, let hunger rather than money guide your decisions.
5. **Office goodies:** Office lunchrooms are stocked full of treats. Appreciative clients and coworkers bring in treats by the armload. Even more food shows up when the holidays approach. At the office, there can be mindless eating booby traps everywhere. Remember that it is great to enjoy food. Give yourself permission to eat something if you really want it. That "I can't have it" attitude sets you up for mindless eating. Anything you can't

have, you are more likely to want. Too often we let guilt guide our actions. If you find yourself mindlessly picking at the treats, leave the room.

6. **Desk dining:** Do you profess that you don't have time for a lunch break? This is unfortunate. As a result, you might multitask while you eat. You can be snacking on some crackers, typing a memo, and talking on your cell phone all at the same time. When you snack while you work, your body doesn't really process what you are eating. Your brain often doesn't fully register the food and you could continue to feel hungry.
7. **Stress eating:** Perhaps you have that dreaded coworker who as they walk down the hall you hear the Darth Vader music beginning to play. People go into hiding and start ducking under desks. The stress reverberates throughout the whole office. Stress eating is a common reason people overeat at work. They don't know what else to do to cope with work stress. Consider alternative ways you can deal with stress at work. Send a quick e-mail. Go for a walk around the cubicles. Take a breather.
8. **Vending machines and morning meetings:** It's 3:00 in the afternoon. There are just two more hours until you get to go home. The vending machines seem to whisper your name and call to you from down the hallway. This is a common temptation. Not to mention the morning meeting with boxes of pastries and donuts. You don't have to always avoid them, just eat them mindfully!

Mindfully Eating at Work Contract

I agree to eat mindfully at work.

I agree not to snack and work at the same time. I'll put down the phone and give eating 100 percent of my attention. When I eat, I'll just eat.

I agree to role model to my coworkers a positive attitude about eating, food, and weight.

I agree to mindfully plan out what I am going to eat each day to avoid getting too hungry, a typical trigger of mindless eating.
I agree to be more aware of the things that prompt me to mindless eating at work.
I agree to acknowledge when I am emotionally eating and try my best to find other ways to manage my stress.
I agree to lose the black and white (all or nothing) thinking. I'll drop the "shoulds" and "musts" in my life and set realistic expectations for myself.
I agree to create a mindful environment. I'll clean off my cubical/desk and remove mindless eating triggers like a candy jar.
I agree to not participate in dieting chitchat around the water cooler. Instead, I agree to talk about mindful eating.
I agree not to base my worth on my looks but focus on doing a good job and feeling proud of my work.
I agree not to police or advise other people regarding their food choices.
I agree not to judge my coworkers based on their size. I also agree not to be competitive or compare myself to my coworkers' bodies.
I agree to continue to practice eating mindfully each and every day. I know that eating mindfully is hard work!

Appendix C

Ten Ways for Campuses to Be More Mindful

1. **Mindful eating days:** Host a Mindful Eating Week, Wellness Fair, Stress Free Zone Day, or create the Bod Squad. Remember to focus these events primarily on teaching positive behaviors. Teach people how to eat mindfully and promote health rather than pointing out problematic behavior. Invite nutritionists, psychologists, yoga instructors, and speakers in on this topic. Make an information table. Give away healthy snacks like energy bars and bottled water.
2. **Create a blog or live journal:** Create a live journal dedicated to mindful eating. Invite your friends to join. Make sure to outline some rules. The journal must focus on encouraging positive changes, not degrading bodies. Start by outlining the principles of mindful eating and invite others to participate in the discussion (www.livejournal.com and www.blogger.com).
3. **Fund raisers and receptions:** Host a formal dance (or sorority/fraternity function) and donate profits to an organization that promotes healthy eating. Remember that sorority women and athletes have an increased risk for eating issues (Hoerr et al. 2002). Why not do something positive, not to mention fun, to help this cause?
4. **Join an advocacy group:** Your club, house, or sorority could apply for a group membership to an association that supports healthy eating. Pick one that frequently sends out fliers and information that you can have on display in your hallway, pass around at chapter meetings, or place on coffee tables for people to read.

Or, for a service project, buy a variety of eating issues books for your women's resource center, the counseling center, or student health center.

5. **Nutrition information:** Many researchers highly recommend increasing nutrition education on campuses (Matvienko et al. 1998). How do you spread the word? One possibility is to form a nutrition awareness campaign. Hang fliers with nutrition information on bathroom doors and in elevators (see www.eatright.org for free pdf downloads on nutrition. Also try www.nutrition.gov/, www.healthyeating.net). Lobby your administration for a healthy eating class or contact your school nutritionist to provide one-two hour workshops.
6. **Art exhibits:** Invite local artists and the art department to create a campus exhibit. Choose a theme related to body image and mindful eating. One artist, for example, donated her body sculptures to be displayed during body image awareness week. Visual arts projects are another medium to help us explore the personal, cultural, and historical dimensions of mindful eating.
7. **Public speakers:** Invite a well-known public speaker on college eating issues. Contact the National Eating Disorders Association for the Speaker's Bureau list. This list contains a number of professionals, celebrities, and individuals who routinely speak on eating issues and promote healthy eating.
8. **Movie night:** This is a great way to stimulate discussion and unwind. Try *Real Women Have Curves, The Stepford Wives, Lovely and Amazing,* and an Italian foreign film called *Melana.*
9. **Great jeans giveaway:** Every year, campuses and eating disorders coalitions around the country encouraged people to donate old pairs of jeans. They urge you to bring your jeans that are too small or the wrong size. The NEDA motto was to feel better about yourself: "Change your JEANS not your GENES!" See www.nationaleatingdisorders.org for more details.
10. **Food and fun:** If you live in an apartment or house, host a "pot luck." Bring a dish that is significant to your culture or family. Maybe it is your mom's secret meatloaf recipe or the turtle brownies you learned to make in Girl Scouts. Tell a story about why

you brought the dish. Or, if you are in a dorm, try a hot chocolate happy hour (only water and hot chocolate mix required). It's the perfect setting to launch a cultural discussion about the sociocultural influence of your campus on health eating. Create a petition with very specific ideas of how the dining services could create a more mindful eating environment. It's important that you share with the administration how you see the school as contributing to the rise in eating issues on campuses today. Also, let the administration know what they are doing that supports mindful eating habits.

Term Paper Topics

Need a term or research paper topic? Interested in learning more about eating issues? Here is a brief list of possible topics. Keep in mind that many of these must be tailored to your particular needs. Talk to your professor for ideas and recommendations.

1. Evaluate eating disorder/body image programs on college campuses. Discuss the challenges, successes, failures, and conclude with your own recommendations.
2. Many insurance companies do not cover or pay for treatment for eating problems and eating disorders. Discuss mental health laws in your state that pertain to this issue (i.e., parity laws).
3. Read a memoir (*Appetites: Why Women Want* by Caroline Knapp; *Good Enough* by Cynthia Nappa Bitter; *"Stick Figure: A Diary of My Former Self"* by Lori Gottlieb; *"Wise Girl"* by Jamie-Lynn Sigler and Sheryl Berk; *"Wasted: A Memoir"* by Marya Hornbacher; *"My Name is Caroline"* by Caroline Adams-Miller; *Food and Loathing: A Lament* by Betsy Lerner; *Slim to None: A Journey Through the Wasteland of Anorexia Treatment* by Jennifer Hendricks). Write a reflection paper or compare and contrast two of the memoirs.
4. Review the personality features that contribute to making an individual "at risk" for an eating issue.
5. Discuss the prevalence rate, developmental factors, and environ-

mental stressors that make college an environment where eating concerns may develop.

6. Review the literature on eating disorders and children. What are some prevention strategies used to address body image in elementary schools?
7. Read *Fast Food Nation* by Eric Schlosser and discuss how fast food and economic conditions contribute to eating problems in America.
8. Examine the research on the connection between childhood sexual abuse and/or sexual assault and the development of eating/body image issues.
9. Read *Good In Bed* by Jennifer Weiner. It's a novel about a woman struggling with her body image. Given the criteria in the *Diagnostic and Statistical Manual of Mental Disorders* (DSM-IV-TR), how would you classify the character's eating issues? What factors in her life significantly impacted her eating/body image issues?
10. College athletes, particularly those sports that emphasize weight restrictions, are at greater risk of eating disorders. Choose a sport or art (ballet, swimming, wrestling, running, etc.) and examine the current literature on one of these areas.
11. Review at least two theories on perfectionist behavior and eating problems.
12. Read *A Starving Madness: Tales of Hunger, Hope, and Healing in Psychotherapy* by Judith Ruskay Rabinor. Go to her Web site www.astarvingmadness.com and respond to the discussion questions.
13. Compare and contrast the effectiveness of psychopharmacological and psychological treatments for bulimia nervosa.
14. Examine the positive and negative influences of the Internet on eating disorders. Discuss the implications and alternatives strategies to dealing with probulimia (Pro-Mia) and proanorexia (Pro-Ana) sites. Comment on how shutting down Web sites of this nature may challenge freedom of speech.
15. Discuss the impact of media (magazine, music videos, and TV ads) on body image. Discuss the ways in which advertising contributes to the problem of eating disorders and body image.
16. The age at which children begin dieting has plummeted over the years. Discuss the prevalence of eating problems in young children.

References

Allison, K., and Park, C. 2004. A prospective study of disordered eating among sorority and nonsorority women. *International Journal of Eating Disorders* 35:354–58.

Anderson, A. 2000. Responding to the phrase "I feel fat." *Eating disorders* 8: 67–69.

Anderson, D., J. Shapiro, and J. Lundgren. 2003. The freshman year of college as a critical period for weight gain: An initial evaluation. *Eating Behaviors* 4:363–67.

Anding, J., R. Suminski, and J. Boss. 2001. Dietary intake, body mass index, exercise and alcohol: Are college women following the dietary guidelines for Americans? *Journal of College Health* 49:167–71.

Baer, R. 2003. Mindfulness training as a clinical intervention: A conceptual and empirical review. *Clinical Psychology: Science and Practice* 10(2):125–43.

Becker, A., D. Franko, K. Nussbaum, and D. Herzog. 2004. Secondary prevention for eating disorders: The impact of education, screening and referral in a college-based screening population. *International Journal of Eating Disorders* 36:157–62.

Bellisle, F., and A. Dalix. 2001. Cognitive restraint can be offset by distraction, leading to increased meal intake in women. *American Journal of Clinical Nutrition* 74(2):97–200.

Burney, J., and H. Irwin. 2000. Shame and guilt in women with eating-disorder symptomology. *Journal of Clinical Psychology* 56(1):51–61.

Cash, T. F. (1995). Developmental teasing about physical appearance: Retrospective descriptions and relationships with body image. *Social Behavior and Personality* 23: 123–30.

Cash, T. F., and J. Hrabosky. 2003. The effects of psychoeducation and self-monitoring in a cognitive-behavioral program for body-image improvement. *Eating Disorders* 11: 255–70.

Cervera, S., F. Lahortiga, M. Martinez-Gonzalez, P. Gual, and A. Irala-Estevez. 2003. Neuroticism and low self-esteem as risk factors for incident eating disorders in a prospective cohort study. *International Journal of Eating Disorders* 33(3):271–80.

Chen H-F, and Holben, D. H. 2000. Changes in weight and body composition of international students new to the US and enrolled in an American University. *Journal of American Dietetic Association.* 100 (Suppl. 1):A-29.

Clayton Pereyra, L. M., M. S. Houston, J. H. Williford Jr., and D. M. Garner. 1997. Eating attitudes, dietary intake, and dieting behaviors in college females. *Journal American Dietetic Association* 97(9) (Suppl):A-48.

Cooley, E, and T. Toray.1996. Disordered eating in college freshman women: A prospective study. *Journal of American College Health* 44:229–35.

Cooley, E., and T. Toray. 2001. Body image and personality predictors of eating disorder symptoms during the college years. *International Journal of Eating Disorders* 30:8–36.

Counihan, CM. 1992. Food rules in the United States: Individualism, control and hierarchy. *Anthropological Quarterly* 65(2):55–67.

Cousineau, T., M. Goldstein, and D. Franko 2004. A collaborative approach to nutrition education for college students. *Journal of American College Health* 53(2):79–83.

Davidson, R., J. Kabat-Zinn, J. Schumacher, M. Rosenkranz, D. Muller, S. Santorelli, F. Urbanowski, A. Harrington, K. Bonus, and J. Sheridan. 2003. Alterations in brain and immune function produced by mindfulness meditation. *Psychosomatic Medicine* 65: 564–70.

Deckro, G., K. Ballinger, M. Hoyt, M. Wilcher, J. Dusek, P. Myers, B. Greensberg, D. Rosenthal, and H. Benson 2002. The evaluation of mind/body interventions to reduce psychological distress and perceived stress in college students. *Journal of American College Health* 50(6):218–87.

DeBate, R. D., M. Topping, and R. G. Sargent. 2001. Racial and gender differences in weight status and dietary practices among college students. *Adolescence* 36(144):819–33.

Eldredge, K., G. T. Wilson, and A. Whaley. 1990. Failure, self-evaluation, and feeling fat in women. *International Journal of Eating Disorders* 9(1):37–50.

Faith, M. S., M. Leone, and D. B., Allison. 1997. The effects of self-generated comparison targets, BMI, and social comparison tendencies on body image appraisal. *Eating Disorders: The Journal of Treatment and Prevention* 5:128–40.

Flipse, R., M. Bradanini, and M. Bradanini. (2002). *Fighting the Freshman Fifteen: A College Woman's Guide to Getting Real about Food and Keeping the Pounds Off.* New York, NY: Random House.

Gilbert, N., and C. Meyer. 2004. Similarities in young women's eating attitudes: Self selected versus artificially constructed groups. *International Journal of Eating Disorders* 36: 213–19.

Gore, S., J. Foster, V. Dillo, K. Kirk, and D. S. West. 2003. Television viewing and snacking. *Eating Behaviors* 4: 399–405.

Graham, M., and A. Jones. 2002. Freshman 15: Valid theory or harmful myth. *Journal of American College Health* 50(4):171–73.

Grassi, A. 2001. The college environment and eating disorders. *Healthy Weight Journal* 15(3): 40–41.

Haberman, S, and D. Luffey. 1998. Weight in college students' diet and exercise behaviors. *Journal of American College Health* 46 (4):189–91.

Hagan, M., J. Tomaka, and D. Moss. 2000. Relation of dieting in college and high school students to symptoms associated with semi-starvation. *Journal of Health Psychology* 5(1): 7–9.

Hausenblas, H., and A. Carron. 1998. Group influences on eating and dieting behaviors in residence members. *College Study Journal* 32(4): 585–89.

Heatherton, T., N. Patricia, F. AM. Mahamedi, and P. A. B., Keel. 1995. Body weight, dieting, and eating disorder symptoms among college students, 1982–1992. *American Journal of Psychiatry* 152(11):1623–29.

Herman, C., D. Roth, and J. Polivy. 2003. Effects of the presence of others on food intake: A normative interpretation. *Psychological Bulletin* 129(6):873–86.

Hess-Biber, S. 1992. Report on a panel longitudinal study of college women's eating patterns and eating disorders. *Health Care Women International* 13:375–91.

Hodge, C. N., L. A. Jackson, and L. A. Sullivan. 1993. The "Freshman 15" facts and fantasies about weight-gain in college women. *Psychology of Women Quarterly* 17:119–26.

Hoerr, S., R. Bokram, B. Lugo, T. Bivins, and D. Keast. 2002. Risk for disordered eting relates to both gender and ethnicity for college students. *Journal of the American College of Nutrition* 21(4):307–14.

Hoyt, W., and S. Ross. 2003. Clinical and subclinical eating disorders in counseling center clinics: A prevalence study. *Journal of College Student Psychotherapy* 17(4):39–54.

Huang, T., K. Harris, R. Lee, N. Nazir, W. Born, and H. Kaur. 2003. Assessing overweight, obesity, diet and physical activity in college students. *Journal of American College Health*52(2):83–86.

Huang.Y., W. O. Song, R. A. Schemmel, and, S. M. Hoerr. 1994. What do college students eat? Food selection and meal patterns. *Nutrition Research* 14(8):1143–53.

Hudd, S., J. Dumlao, D. Erdmann-Sager, D. Murray, E. Phan, N. Soukas, and N. Yokozuka. 2000. Stress at college: Effects on health habits, health status and self-esteem. *College Student Journal* 34(2):217–34.

Hudd, S., J. Dumlao, D. Erdmann-Sager, D. Murray, E. Phan, N. Soukas, N. Yokozuka. 2000. Stress at college: Effects on health habits, health status and self-esteem. *College Student Journal* 34(2): 21–31.

Jacobi, C. 2005. Psychosocial risk factors for eating disorders. *Eating Disorder Review*, ed. Wonderlich, S., J. Mitchell, M. De Zwann, and H. Steiger, Part I. Oxford: Radcliffe Publishing.

Jones, N.,and P. Rogers. 2003. Preoccupation, food and failure: An investigation of cognitive performance deficits in dieters. *International Journal of Eating Disorders* 33(2): 185–92.

Kabat-Zinn, J. 1990. *Full Catastrophe Living: Using the Wisdom of Your Body and Mind to Face Stress, Pain and Illness*. New York: Dell.

Kabat-Zinn, J., A. O. Massion, J. Kristeller et al. 1992. Effectiveness of a meditation-based stress reduction program in the treatment of anxiety disorders. *American Journal of Psychiatry* 149:936–43.

Kitsantas, A., T. Gilligan, and A. Kamata. 2003. College women with eating disorders: self-regulation, life satisfaction, and positive/negative affect. *Journal of Psychology* 137(4): 381–95.

Kristeller, J. L., and C. B. Hallett. 1999. An exploratory study of meditation-based intervention for binge eating disorder. *Journal of Health Psychology* 4:357–63.

Levitsky, D., C. Halbmaier, and G. Mrdjenovic. 2004. The freshman weight gain: a model for the study of the epidemic of obesity. *International Journal of Obesity* 28(11): 1435–442.

Levitsky, D., and T. Youn. 2003. The more food young adults are served, the more they overeat. *Journal of Nutrition* 134:2546–549.

Linehan, M. 1993. *Cognitive-Behavioral Treatment for Borderline Personality Disorder*. New York: Guilford Press.

Ma, J., N. M. Betts, T. Horacek, C. Georgiou, A. White, and S. Nitzke. 2002. The importance of decisional balance and self efficacy in relation to stages of change for fruit and vegetable intakes by young adults. *American Journal of Health Promotion* 16 (3):157–66.

Matvienko, O., D. Lewis, and E. Schafer. 2001. A college nutrition science rouse as an intervention to prevent weight gain in female college freshman. *Journal of Nutritional Education* 33: 95–101.

McFarlane, T., J. Polivy, and R. McCabe.1999. Help, not harm: psychological foundation for nondieting approach toward health. *Journal of Social Issues* 55(2):261–76.

Mintz, L. B., and N. E. Betz. 1988. Prevalence and correlates of eating disorders behaviors among college students. *Journal of Counseling Psychology* 3:463--71.

Murphy, R., S. Frost, P. Webster, and U. Schmidt. 2004. An evaluation of web-based information. *International Journal of Eating Disorders* 35:145–54.

Nash, J. 1999. *Binge no more*. Berkeley, CA: New Harbinger.

Netz Y., and R. Lidor. 2003. Mood alterations in mindful versus aerobic exercise modes. *The Journal of Psychology* 137(5):405–19.

O'Dea, J., and S. Abraham. 2002. Eating and exercise disorders in young college men. *Journal of American College Health* 50(6):273–78.

Olivardia, R., H. Pope, B. Mangweth, and J. Hudson. 1995. Eating disorders in college men. *American Journal of Psychiatry* 152(9):1279–85.

Painter, J., Wansink, B. and Hieggelke, J. B. 2002, How visibility and convenience influence candy consumption. *Appetite* 38:237–38.

Parham, E., J. Lennon, and M. Kolosi. 2001. Do all college students have eating disorders? *Healthy Weight Journal* 15(3):366–70.

Putterman, E., and W. Linden. 2004. Appearance versus health: Does the reason for the diet affect dieting behavior. *Journal of Behavioral Medicine* 27(2):185–204.

Prinz, P. 2004. Sleep, appetite, and obesity—What is the link? *PLoS Med* 1(3):e61. http://www.plosjournals.org.

Pyle, R., P. Neuman, P. Halvorson, and J. Mitchell. 1991. An ongoing cross-sectional study of the prevalence of eating disorders in freshman college students. *International Journal of Eating Disorders* 10(6):667–77.

Racette, S., S. Deusinger, M. Strube, G. Highstein, and R. Deusinger. 2005. Weight changes, exercise, and dietary patterns during freshman and sophomore years of college. *Journal of American College Health* 53(6):245–51.

Reibel, D. K., J. M. Greeson, G. S. Brainard, and, S. Rosenzweig. 2001. Mindfulness-based stress reduction and health related quality of life in heterogeneous patient populations. *General Hospital Psychiatry* 23:183–92.

Rodin, J., R. Striegel-Moore, and L. Silberstein. 1990. "Vulnerability and resilience in the age of eating disorders: risk and protective factors for bulimia nervosa." In *Risk and protective factors in the development of psychopathology,* ed. Jon Rolf et al., 361–83. New York: Cambridge University Press.

Rosenzweig, S., D. Reibel, J. Greeson, G. Brainard, and M. Hojat. 2003. Mindfulness-based stress reduction lowers psychological distress in medical students. *Teaching and Learning in Medicine* 15(2):88–92.

Rozin, P, R. Bauer, and D. Catanese. 2003. Food and life, pleasure and worry, among American college students: Gender differences and regional similarities. *Journal of Personality & Social Psychology* 85(1):132–41.

Safer D.L., C. F. Telch, and W. S. Agras. 2001. Dialectical behavior therapy for bulimia nervosa: a case study. *International Journal of Eating Disorders* 30:101–106.

Schwitzer, A., L. Rodriguez, C. Thomas, and L. Salimi. 2001. The eating disorder NOS diagnostic profile among college women. *Journal of American College Health* 49:157–66.

Segal, Z. V., J.M.G. Willams, and J. D. Teasdale. 2001. *Mindfulness-Based Cognitive Therapy for Depression.* New York: Guildford Press.

Shapiro, SL., GE., Schwartz., G. Bonner, 1998. Effects of Mindfulness-based stress reduction on medical and premedical students. *Journal of Behavioral Medicine* 21:581–99.

Shisslak, C. M., M. Crago, and L. S. Estes. 1995. The spectrum of eating disturbances. *International Journal of Eating Disorders* 18(3):209–19.

Snelling, A, M. Schaeffer, and S. Lehrhoff. 2002. Dieting and nutritional patterns of college females. *Implications for College Health Educators* 33(6):357–61.

Stice, E., J. Maxfield, and T. Wells. 2003. Adverse effects of social pressure to be thin on young women: An experiment to be thin on young women: An experimental investigation of the effects of fat talk." *International Journal of Eating Disorders* 34(1):108–117.

Striegel-Moore, R., G. McAvay, and J. Rodin. 1986. Psychological and behavioral correlates of feeling fat in women. *Journal of Eating Disorders* 5(5):935–47.

Strohmetz, D, B. Rind, R. Fisher, and M. Lynn. 2002. Sweetening the till: The use of candy to increase restaurant tipping. *Journal of Applied Social Psychology* 32(2):300–309.

Teasdale, J.D., Z. V. Segal, J. M. G. Williams. et al. 2000. Prevention of relapse/recurrence in major depression by mindfulness-based cognitive therapy. *Journal of Consulting and Clinical Psychology* 68:615–23.

Thompson, J. K., M. D. Coovert, and S. M. Stormer. 1999. Body image, social comparison, and eating disturbance: A covariance structure modeling investigation. *International Journal of Eating Disorders* 26:43–51.

Tiggemann, M., and B. McGill. 2004a. The role of social comparison in the effect of magazine advertisements on women's mood and body dissatisfaction. *Journal of Social and Clinical Psychology* 23(1):23–44.

Tiggemann, M,. and A. Slater. 2004b. Thin ideals in music television: A source of social comparison and body dissatisfaction. *International Journal of Eating Disorders* 35(1): 48–58.

Torte, M., and P. Cornelissen. 2001. Female and male perceptions of female physical attractiveness in front-view and profile. *British Journal of Psychology* 92(2):391–402.

Tylka, T., and M. L. Subich. 2004. Examining a multidimensional model of eating disorder symptomatology among college women. *Journal of Counseling Psychology* 51(3):314–28.

Vohs, K., T. Heatherton, and M. Herrin. 2001. Disordered eating and the transition to college: a prospective study. *International Journal of Eating Disorders* 29:280–88.

Wansink, B., M. Cheney, and N. Chan. 2003. Exploring comfort foods preferences across age and gender. *Physiology and Behavior* 79:739–47.

Weingarten, H., and D. Elston. 1991. Food cravings in a college population. *Appetite* 17(3):167–75.

Wisniewski, L., and E. Kelly. 2003. Can DBT be used to effectively treat eating disorders? *Cognitive and Behavioral Practice* 10:131–38.

About the Author

Dr. Susan Albers
Author photo by Jeffrey Neumann

Susan Albers Psy.D. is a psychologist and author of *Eating Mindfully: How to End Mindless Eating and Develop a Balanced Relationship with Food.* She obtained her doctorate from the University of Denver and completed a postdoctoral fellowship at Stanford University. She has worked and trained at the University of Colorado in Boulder, the University of Notre Dame, Ohio Wesleyan University, and the Cleveland Clinic Foundation. She specializes in counseling college students with eating and relationship issues. Her work has been noted in *O the Oprah Magazine* and *Alternative Medicine*. She conducts mindful eating workshops across the country and internationally. Visit her Web site at www.mindfuleating101.com.